MW01528372

ADVANCE PRAISE

"*God's Not Done with You is such a refreshing and inspiring read. I loved Mary's style of writing—so relatable—and, wow, so many examples of exactly what I have personally experienced. The process of creating one's plan can seem daunting, but she walks us through and provides encouragement, expertise, and some help via God's presence to realize I CAN do this! It's through your guidance that we (women) are able to recognize our purest form and potential. This is the book you will be telling your girlfriends to read next.*"

—Brooke Owen, Career Development Assistant and Mentoring Program Coordinator at Pennsylvania State University

"*Mary Guirovich taps into the soul of powerful, high-performance, professional women within the first two pages. Through the book, she lights the way for so many who are sitting back quietly and accepting their fate. Read the book. Put into action what you learn in the book. Then take the world by storm!*"

—Jessica S. Andrews, Director of Operations at Advance Your Reach, LLC

"In God's Not Done with You, Mary Guirovich has been able to eloquently, thoughtfully, and powerfully bring together a wonderful mix of research-driven strategies that will not only position women for advancement professionally but that also lay out a blueprint for thriving personally and spiritually. I truly believe she has found a winning recipe to help women create the life that God is calling them to live, both personally and professionally, through stories and guidance that capture the reader's heart and mind in a phenomenal way!"

—Daphne Valcin, corporate trainer and coach

"If you're a woman of faith who wants to take the next step in your career and live your life in abundance, you need God's Not Done with You. Mary powerfully shares how you can reach your God-given potential in your career without sacrificing your faith in the process. Mary's story is truly inspiring and will have you experiencing more divine joy, peace, and fulfillment in your career in no time."

—Nicole Andrews, Founder and CEO of Nicole Andrews International Career Coaching and Speaking

"God's Not Done with You—the title alone connects the two most important people we know...God, our sovereign Creator, and ourselves, which means YOU—His crown of creation. Mary has captured the essence of a Christ-filled, abundant life we can live through His grace and mercy. Her willingness to go there, vulnerability, and transparency render every aspect of this book's content completely relatable to the reader. Immerse yourself in this book, and He will transform your life!"

—Ken Sharrar, Director, Mission Advancement Director at John Paul the Great Catholic University

"Powerful and thought-provoking! Mary Guirovich addresses many issues that women face while also reminding us we're not alone and God's not done with us yet! If you're looking to find clarity in your calling, read this book!"

—Kim Rich, author of *Rich Lessons*

"Mary has written a must-read for anyone who believes that 'plans of the diligent lead to profit as surely as haste leads to poverty' (Proverbs 21:5, NIV). Read the book, and plan your promotion with the intent to increase your family household income unapologetically."

—Loeka Wiltz, MBA, Co-founder of Atknho.org and certified small business commercialization technologist

MARY E. GUIROVICH

GOD'S *Not Done* WITH YOU

How to Advance
Your Career and
Live in Abundance

GOD'S NOT DONE WITH YOU

How to Advance Your Career and Live In Abundance

ISBN 978-1-5445-2578-5 *Hardcover*
978-1-5445-2576-1 *Paperback*
978-1-5445-2577-8 *Ebook*

To God, for planting the seed of this book inside of me long ago.

For my Pastor, Dr. Ed Newton, for watering the seed through your unapologetic sermons.

For the blood of Jesus that has saved me and brought me peace through a relationship with God.

To the Holy Spirit, who helped this book grow into something greater than my wildest dreams.

And to Mariza. God's not done with you.

CONTENTS

PART 3: TRANSFORMING YOUR CAREER

PREFACE

CONFESSIONS FROM A CHRISTIAN WORKAHOLIC

I was running on all cylinders, taking coaching calls as I prepared for the day and as I drove my kids to school in the early morning hours. In the evening, my husband, Louis, would call to check on me and to see if I would be missing family dinner once again. My life was run by my schedule. If my kids or spouse happened to forget to tell me about an event, I wouldn't attend if it meant canceling a work event. Although, if an emergency work event emerged, I would cancel my personal plans, no questions asked. I know some of you are already thinking, *What a crappy mom*. And you're right. I was a crappy mom, wife, friend, and Christian sometimes. I didn't get it all right, and it came with consequences.

After giving birth to my fourth child, I received a raise that I wasn't proud of. This did a lot of damage to my psyche. On the outside, it looked like I was on the fast track. I was named team member of the year, had the largest and most successful coaching load. I had been recently promoted to Service Operations Manager. My role was to train and develop new coaches, improve overall client outcomes, and ensure a top-notch customer service experience for the hundreds of clinic owners and their teams that we worked with.

I was working hard to be noticed—dreaming of climbing the corporate ladder to the top. Being on top would mean success, power, titles, perks, and freedom. But all my hard work only earned me more work. More work equated to gobs of stress, and it left me throwing what little self-care I had preserved out the window.

When I was in this low moment, I considered leaving the company and getting my teaching certificate. I contemplated going back to school to up my game. I tried going part-time to enjoy life more, but I worked just as hard for even less money.

Everything I was experiencing was my fault. I thought that if I worked hard enough, I would get noticed and compensated for it. But I was uncomfortable advocating for myself and minimized the value of my abilities.

The couple times I mustered up the courage to ask for a raise, I went about it all wrong. Then when I was given a raise, it was below what I thought I deserved. I didn't express what I really thought about how much value I added to the company. Why? Because I didn't know my value. This left me bitter and resentful.

The truth is, most companies consider managers successful when they get the highest quality work at the lowest possible price. That's called doing good business in the eyes of the secular world. If you have been settling for the company's standard 3 percent and below raises like I used to do, you can be assured that others ask for more and get it. It's not necessarily because they are better employees but because they value themselves and have the courage to communicate that value.

Things started to change in 2016 when I made a decision not to have another manager leading me that I trained. I told my manager at a leadership meeting that I would be the next Chief Operating Officer. I wasn't kicking them out, but mentally I had decided that I wanted it. For the first time, I believed that I could do it.

Little did I know the position would open up a few months later. I didn't know for certain if I would succeed, but I knew that it was my turn to try. So I went into the manager's office and let him know I wanted the position.

But he didn't give me the position. He said that I would have to perform the responsibilities of the position before I could get the title and pay. This felt like an impossible task. The team didn't want to be led, much less by me. One person told me they didn't like women managers, another said that I acted like a union rep, and others would simply disregard me.

This wasn't shocking, as I wasn't their manager, and most people don't like change. I did have a few fans and the support of the founder. But needless to say, it wasn't working.

One day I sat alone at work on my day off, pondering what to do. I wanted so badly to lead the team. I could clearly see where we were going wrong, and I had ideas, but I struggled to communicate them verbally.

That's when my husband called me and said that he thought his company was going in a different direction and he would be out of his job of twenty years. My heart sank as I absorbed the reality of the situation. My husband, the breadwinner, was going to be out of a job, and I was incapable of earning a promotion. I did what any loving wife would do and told him that everything was going to be ok. God had given me an idea to outline my vision for the company on paper.

For the next few weeks, I went to work brainstorming and writing down all of my ideas. Some of them were from problems I noticed and others from past experiences. I could envision how things could be, but I needed to transfer that vision.

A few weeks later, I turned in what I now call the My Promotion Plan to the founder and CEO. At that point, I felt like I had nothing to lose.

I was made Vice President of Operations the next day. Through promotion planning, I went on to become the Chief Operating Officer, a partner, was told I was on track to be CEO in one to two years, and was encouraged to start a personal leadership business.

By completing the My Promotion Plan, my confidence, career, company, and lifestyle have been transformed. Every day, I performed work that was fulfilling. I had the opportunity to coach hundreds of functional medicine practitioners and thousands of team members across the globe. Together we worked to revolutionize healthcare from the traditional sick care model that we are most familiar with today to a new model where the patient is empowered through education on how their body can reverse or prevent chronic disease.

I led the most incredible team of people, and we continually worked together to provide the best experience, learning tools, and outcomes for our clients. Leading our team and the company and making a difference in the lives of thousands of people couldn't be more rewarding.

As you'll see in this book, I believe God gave me the tools to succeed. But it's only through the Holy Spirit that I have renewed my heart and mind in a way that truly transformed me, my life, and my career. I've worked hard to examine the motives of my heart and surrender to the Lord. Where I used to depend on my ability and excessive amounts of hard work to climb the corporate ladder, today I live surrendered to God's will to encourage my children, spouse, and clients. I learned to love myself and others unconditionally and to lead with a servant's heart, allowing me to experience the abundance of God's promises.

INTRODUCTION

YOUR STARTING POINT

Do you believe that you are capable of leading a company—the one you are working for now?

There was a time I didn't believe I could. I was stuck—until I believed. Before I became an executive, I didn't realize the importance of believing in myself and my abilities. But even if you know you're good enough and you believe in yourself, you still have to do it.

The My Promotion Plan process I'm about to teach you is straightforward—and proven to work. But the perfect plan isn't what's holding you back from earning the promotion that you want. What's holding you back is much deeper.

Right now, as you read this book, you might be hoping that it will be the silver bullet that lands you in the career of your dreams. You might be hoping that it takes all of your troubles away. Or maybe you're hoping for a simple script to get your manager to give you a raise.

To be successful in anything, we need more than the perfect system or script. Before a system can work, we must believe in ourselves. As women of faith, we need an unwavering trust in God, who has given us the capacity and His strength to be more than we can imagine. We need to trust that God has already given us everything through the death, burial, and resurrection of Jesus. We need to surrender our understanding in order to experience being the women God intended for us to be by doing things that are not always logical, comfortable, or in line with what we "feel like" doing.

So how does this impact our careers and our desire to advance?

Sadly, too many women haven't been supported in their attempt to answer this question. As a result, they live far below their true potential, no matter how hard they work or how long they wait. Their true potential remains hidden inside, and the life of abundance they were created to live in is never realized. Many of us have asked the following questions:

Doesn't God want me to be grateful for what I already have?

Should I even want to work outside the home while raising kids or supporting a family?

How am I going to keep up with the demands of today's world?

Does it matter if I make less than men earn for doing the same work?

If my spouse is the breadwinner, does my income matter that much?

Won't the Lord provide my daily bread?

Is it ok to desire more money?

Isn't God supposed to give me the promotion?

Do I need to go back to school?

If I'm not valued here, should I get another job?

What if they find out I'm an imposter and I'm not as good as they thought?

Am I enough?

And how many of us have had these thoughts?

My manager hasn't given me a raise, even though I've had great reviews. I must not be ready.

Others around me are advancing, and they don't do a fraction of what I do.

I can't ask for a raise. I don't want to be viewed as one of those entitled millennials.

Since starting to write this book and through my online My Promotion Plan course, I've heard so many stories about women haunted by such thoughts and questions but didn't have the confidence or know-how to go about advancing their careers. I started teaching others the My Promotion Plan system, leading to their own promotions and raises.

Many women know deep down that they are made for more, but their minds are holding them back from having the courage to go out and get what they want. This book will give you practical steps to help you gain the confidence and plan you need to advance your career. You will learn what God says you are capable of and how to use His strength as yours.

My goal is to teach you the best way to set career advancement goals so that your mind can get busy achieving them.

YOU DESERVE TO LIVE YOUR DREAM LIFE IF YOU BELIEVE IT.

DOUBT CREEPS IN

Meet Elizabeth. She is like many of the women that I've mentored across the country.

Elizabeth nailed her last project, and her company has been elevated.

Her manager calls her into his office, and she is on cloud nine. Thinking that she has finally tipped the scales after many successful projects, she even lets herself believe she's going to get the raise and promotion she has worked so hard for. She enters the office with a smile on her face, and her shoulders pulled back. She sits in the black leather chair with her ankles crossed as she smiles at her manager.

"Elizabeth, you did a nice job closing out that project. It is going to make a huge impact. I'd like you to work on something else for me. We are having an issue with a top client's account, and I think you're the person for the job. Are you up to it?"

With an already thinly stretched schedule and her home life bursting at the seams, she grins once more and says, "I'd be honored to help with the account."

Her manager replies with enthusiasm: "Great, I'd like to get an update on your plan by the end of the week."

Leaving the office, she heads straight for the bathroom. The tears start to form in her eyes. Excitement has transformed into resentment and frustration.

As she sits in the bathroom, she wonders, *Where did I go wrong? Why am I never good enough? Why didn't I ask for more money? Why doesn't he advance me like others? If I can't get promoted here, will I have to find another job? Is this really what God wants for my life?*

Elizabeth wipes her final tears, takes a deep breath, straightens her outfit, lifts her head, and fakes a smile as she emerges from the bathroom. She has no choice but to complete the project she committed to. She quickly starts to plan accordingly and tells herself, *This is the last time. When you nail this project, you are not going to sit around and wait any longer. You're going in there to ask for what you deserve.*

She nails the next project.

But doubt creeps in. She starts to think, *Maybe I'm not that good anyway. If my manager doesn't have enough confidence in me to promote me, maybe I'm just not ready. Reviews will be here in six months. I'll ask then.*

Elizabeth represents the majority of women in the workforce

today—hardworking, dedicated, and high-achieving but too often without the compensation and titles to match.

YOUR TIME IS NOW

As a manager and executive, I've had the privilege of interviewing and hiring many new team members. I've hired many talented people, people who couldn't earn promotions after years of work in their previous roles. I can't imagine that they had a mystical burst of personal growth overnight. This left me perplexed because I was taught not to hire people who couldn't get promoted at their previous jobs. So I dug deeper and discovered that there was an epidemic of women that were working hard and waiting to be noticed. But they weren't putting their hands up because they deeply desired to be noticed, didn't know their value, or questioned if they were capable.

Shortly after starting my leadership business and realizing that I wasn't the only one who struggled with the confidence and the know-how to advance, I knew that I wanted to help people advance in their careers. It just so happened that all my clients ended up being Christian women. On our weekly group coaching calls, women would ask if they should try to advance if they want to have a child, or another. They questioned the timing of asking for a promotion after needing to care for their parents' medical needs and calling off one day. They questioned if their ideas were good enough. If *they* were enough. They questioned if God wanted them to work.

That's when I knew that I wanted to work more with women. But after writing the manuscript of this book, God spoke to me, saying, "Mary, I'm supposed to be in this book." As a recovering perfectionist, I assumed this was a made-up delay tactic to postpone the editing portion, which I felt ill-equipped to tackle. So I decided to ask Emily, my editor. Surely, she would tell me that this was a bad idea and to just get on with the editing. But she didn't. She told me that I should, in fact, put God in my book because she could tell that my faith has been a vital part of who I am.

She was right. I found it difficult not to bring my faith in because my relationship with the Lord is the very reason that I have the ability to have written this book. The Lord is the ultimate CEO and the one that provides all my needs. All of our work in and outside the home is to be done for the glory of God.

WORK IS WORSHIP.

I wasn't perfect at this part every step of the way, and there were many times when I tried to manipulate and take the reins. Each time this would happen, I would become filled with anxiety and worry—living a life far from the one God designed for me. God wants the best for you, and apart from God, pure peace doesn't exist.

THE JOURNEY AHEAD

This book is broken down into three parts. Part 1: A Woman's Place; Part 2: Harmonizing Your Heart and Renewing Your Mind; and Part 3: Transforming Your Career.

In Part 1: A Woman's Place, we time travel to the Garden of Eden to discover God's plan for women. We discuss the challenges and facts that women have faced and are facing in their career advancement journeys through to the present day. This background is important for understanding why we think and feel the way we do about career advancement as women.

Because there have been many great books written on the extensive challenges women face when working toward career advancement, I don't cover the entire history of the gender parity gap. There is no denying that implicit bias affects all women at work and in life. The most energizing and powerful thing I've learned from studying these texts is that women are incredibly competent in any area they choose.

In Part 2: Harmonizing Your Heart and Renewing Your Mind, we explore how to align the mind with the heart to bring authentic peace to your life while gaining clarity on your true heart's desires for your life. Most women harbor negative feelings, thoughts, and beliefs that create limits in what is possible for their lives, causing them to miss out on the life God intended for them to live while on Earth. You will learn how to remove limiting beliefs, fully embrace your inheritance as a child of God, and naturally reduce stress.

In Part 2, I've added sections called Actions Taken in Faith, which will accompany each chapter. These sections are a summary of action items for each chapter. Reading a book or taking a course can only change your life if you put into action what you learn. You may not fully grasp a concept until it is implemented, and you may even doubt the actions will work for you. When I first discovered the concepts in this book, I didn't know how they would impact my life. But after implementing and adjusting the concepts, my results have exceeded my wildest dreams. I've never experienced more peace, love, joy, hope, and abundance in my life. My greatest hope is that you find peace in your career advancement journey and life by implementing your Actions Taken in Faith consistently.

In Part 3: Transforming Your Career, you will gain an understanding of common career mistakes. If you have asked for raises and promotions in the past like I did and fell short, then knowing what not to do is often as important as knowing what to do.

Then we cover the complete step-by-step instructions on how to create your own My Promotion Plan that makes your manager say, "That's impressive. I have to do something for this person." Follow these steps, and by the end of the book, you will have your My Promotion Plan in hand.

You'll learn how to conduct your career advancement meeting by following a simple outline. This meeting goes hand in hand with your plan to ensure you are set up for rapid implementation.

Lastly, we'll look at how to live in your new reality and ensure that you get the results you want year after year—so you can overcome your fears and get on with the life of your dreams.

During this process, you won't have to compromise your values or risk damaging relationships by using tactics that threaten your manager. You will learn how to embrace the plan that the Lord has for you—allowing you to live life in the present moment with confidence, peace, and love.

This book explores some essential psychological, emotional, and physical concepts to help you understand the transformative process I want to encourage you to pursue. (I spare you the scientific jargon that might leave you feeling lost and confused.)

Most importantly, this book is designed to help you unlock your God-given potential, grow closer to God, and make a difference in your career, your company, and your family through learning how to create and implement a My Promotion Plan. If you follow the steps and timelines outlined, you can experience the same results as other women—a life where you know you are living at your highest potential.

This is your chance to be the change you wish to see in the world. Before we can help others, we must help ourselves. If you want to help other women and make a real impact on the gender parity gap, then the time is now for you to declare, "God's not done with me."

Part 1

A WOMAN'S PLACE

CHAPTER 1

CAREER ADVANCEMENT 101

Your formal education was missing the one class that would set you up for a lifetime of success—Career Advancement 101. Career Advancement 101 probably wasn't offered at the high school, college, or university you went to. It's as if career advancement is supposed to happen by simply taking a preset path or following the company's rules. It seems so simple. Why would we need to learn how to advance our careers? Why can't we just get a step-by-step playbook to follow?

Because career advancement is complicated.

If there is a standard playbook for career advancement, there are at least a few problems that we'll inevitably encounter. Different companies have different playbooks. Companies ignore their playbooks. Managers have invisible playbooks, often in their head. Added to all that, the people managing the playbook interpret the playbooks differently without even knowing it, meaning few employees have ever read the book or understand the plays. And then there's the fact that the same playbook isn't used for men and women, and the odds are in favor of men. But nobody believes that the women are in a disadvantaged position, leaving the spectators giving well-intended but faulty advice.[1]

Beyond the lack of knowledge on how to advance one's career, our society doesn't support men and women equally when it comes to family life. A man is generally given one week of paternity leave, if any time off at all. Society and companies have declared that it's a woman's job to raise children. There is a lack of support for new moms who medically need to care for their babies through breastfeeding. Moms are deemed to be less available after having children, whereas men are seen as being more responsible. Yet, most companies don't give women less work or lower their expectations when they become mothers.[2]

Women typically have less time to devote to their careers outside of working hours than men, 39 percent of whom do not have a working spouse. In the US, 81 percent of single parents are mothers, and more single working mothers live in poverty than men.[3] For women who are married, there's often household chore inequality. Surveys show that men do about 40 percent of the work, while women do 60 percent of the work in the home because the house's cleanliness is not expected of them socially.[4]

Women also are expected to keep up certain appearances professionally, for whom a more professional appearance has been linked with higher wages. This is a two-fold problem: additional grooming takes an average of fifty-five minutes a day, and the cost of products to maintain a polished appearance has a pink tax. Studies show that products marketed to women that are comparable to men's products cost 42 percent more.[5] That means more time and more money are required to earn a higher income. And even if nobody is talking about it, implicit beauty bias is real.

Society has subconsciously determined what men's work and women's work is, which can be easily demonstrated by doing a quick gender bias exercise. Read each profession and take note of which gender your mind automatically goes to: engineer, construction worker, nurse, teacher, baseball player, secretary, lawyer, hairdresser, and CEO. When people hear the professions engineer, construction worker, baseball player, lawyer, and CEO, they most often think of a man first. When they hear a nurse, teacher, secretary, and hairdresser, they typically think of a woman first.

Our society has shaped these perceptions, and without even thinking, we categorize people accordingly. It's part of our internal wiring. But when it comes to career advancement, the burden falls on women.

These issues are generally seldom addressed within organizations because the owners and managers don't believe that they are, in fact, biased. They truly believe that they are picking the most qualified or best person for the position. Trying to breach a conversation with a man on gender diversity is likely to feel like a personal attack and has been shown to backfire.

Currently, only 21 percent of executive positions are held by women, even though women make up more than half of the workforce and have more educational degrees than men on all levels. On average, women are paid 20 percent less than men for doing similar work.[6] Gains are being made and companies that are embracing diversity are reaping the benefits with high profits. But there's a long way to go.

THE ISSUE OF GENDER EQUALITY ISN'T A MAN'S ISSUE OR A WOMAN'S ISSUE. IT'S A HUMAN ISSUE—A HUMAN ISSUE THAT HAS CASCADING EFFECTS ON OUR ECONOMY.

When a woman is paid less at work, she receives lower social security benefits, has less disposable income to invest, and her average raise will be less. With fewer resources and more responsibility, the gap in a woman's quality of life quickly diminishes if she doesn't have a spouse to offset the compensation gap.

So how is it that we got here in the first place?

CHAPTER 2

A BRIEF HISTORY OF WOMEN'S CAREER ADVANCEMENT

Why are women paid less than men for doing the same job? Why is it that women fill less than a quarter of the seats at the executive table?

How did we arrive at this point in a country that stands for equality and freedom? In a country with laws that demand fair pay for work regardless of race, sex, nationality, or religion? To understand a woman's role and how we arrived at the present reality, we will explore four areas:

1. God's design for women
2. The Industrial Revolution
3. Laws that support women at work
4. Our culture's impact

To appreciate the full picture, let's start at the beginning. You don't need to be a theologian to explore whether God wants women to work or not. It's a question many of my clients ask today, along with questions about career advancement and seeking promotions if they're going to have a family. Let's take a look at God's plan.

GOD'S DESIGN FOR WOMEN

In the beginning, God created woman and man in His image. Genesis 1:27 states, "So God created mankind in his own image, in the image of God he created them; male and female he created them."

We were created to have dominion over all of creation, as it says in Genesis 1:28: "God blessed them and said to them, 'Be fruitful and increase in number; fill the earth and subdue it. Rule over the fish in the sea and the birds in the sky and over every living creature that moves on the ground.'"

Although men and women are created with different features, we were both designed to work together to take care of everything under the sun. This includes taking care of our families and taking care of the world. Genesis 2:18 states, "The Lord God said, 'It is not good for the man to be alone. I will make a helper suitable for him.'"

This verse has caused a lot of controversy because the words "helper" and "suitable" are used. Helper was translated from the Hebrew word *ezer*, which is used twenty-one times in the Old Testament. Twice, it refers to women; three times, it was in reference to military support; and the remaining sixteen times, it is used to describe God. R. David Freedman wrote that the word *ezer* originally had two roots: "to rescue, to save," and "to be strong."[7]

When we understand the word *ezer* is more powerful than the traditional meaning of a helper, we can understand that women were not created merely to work as a man's assistant. In fact, *ezer* is never used in a secondary role but rather in a superior or equal position. Women were not created to serve men.

WE WERE CREATED TO SERVE WITH MEN. GOD HAS GIVEN WOMEN THE SAME DESCRIPTOR THAT HE GAVE HIMSELF!

The Hebrew word *kenegdo* means "opposite as to him" or "corresponding as to him." Being complementary is something that you are—it is not something that you do or become.[8] Victor Hamilton describes it as: "[Kenegdo] suggests that what God creates for Adam will correspond to him. Thus the new creation will be neither a superior nor an inferior, but an equal. The creation of this helper will form one-half of a polarity and will be to man as the South Pole is to the North Pole."[9]

Chayil is another word that has been translated inconsistently. In the English Standard Version (ESV), when *chayil* is translated to describe men, it's translated as "valor," "valiant warriors," "mighty man of valor," "army," "valiant men," but when *chayil* is translated regarding women, the meaning changes to "virtuous," "chaste," "excellent, noble."[10] The Free Dictionary defines valor as the qualities of a hero or heroine; exceptional or heroic courage when facing danger (especially in battle). *Chayil* is meant to represent someone in God's army who is strong, courageous, powerful, valiant, and a warrior, regardless of gender.

Between the word *ezer* and the word *chayil*, God continually uses military terms to describe women. You are meant to be on the front lines. You are meant to be courageous for Christ. You are a strength, a force to be reckoned with.

In this sense, God didn't tell women only to take care of work at home, in the same way that He never instructed men not to care for their homes and families.

When the earth was originally formed, everything that was created was good. Everything was lush, green, and food was abundant. Everything, including the animals, lived in perfect harmony. God's plan was Heaven on Earth, and today God still wants us to experience life as He intended. God didn't create us to control us. He made us with free will. He wants us to desire a relationship with Him not because He demands us to, but because we deeply desire to.

When Adam and Eve ate the forbidden fruit, sin was introduced into the world. This sin was not from God. God didn't tempt Adam or Eve—the Serpent did. But the Serpent didn't cause them to sin; they did that out of their own free will. The Serpent told Eve that their eyes would be opened and they would be like God if they ate from the tree of the knowledge of good and evil. God had already given them everything but the fruit of that single tree. Adam and Eve fell to temptation, and the world would never be the same.

Due to the Fall, we started to experience lack for the first time, and evil entered the world in many forms in order to satisfy that feeling. Patriarchy wasn't created according to God's laws. It came after the Fall. This isn't because God changed. We did.

Although God created us in His image and has a plan for us, we still each play a part. Free will exists, and often we are enticed by the things of this world, causing us to sin. People sin because they do not believe they can get what they desire without sinning. Much like Eve, we, too, don't believe in what God has already promised and freely given to us.

Over the years, people continued to sin, but some people chose to follow God and trust Him. These are the people that God uses and places His favor in because they have a heart after the Lord. Abraham, Moses, David, and Daniel are a few well-known men. Esther, Ruth, Lydia, Mary, and Phoebe are a few well-known women. With God, seemingly ordinary people can do incredible things. Not because they are incredible, but because they have the strength of God. Not because they are sinless, but because they (men and women) have a desire to do God's will.

In the Bible, we are given examples of women who do *ezer* work.

The Proverbs 31 woman, for example, is an eager worker; she does hard work, she works long hours, she is a mother, she provides for her family, she provides for her crew, she is a property owner, she is an investor, she sets about her work vigorously, she is equipped with skill for her tasks, she values her work, she is not in need, she has luxuries, she engages her work, she gives to the poor, she helps the needy with her hands, she does not live in fear, she provides for her family's basic needs, she is fashionable, she speaks highly of her husband, she is in direct sales, she understands marketing, she is in wholesale, she has dignity, she enjoys life, she is educated, she leads others with her instruction, she watches the affairs of her household, she does not seek handouts due to inactivity, her children see her as blessed, her husband acknowledges her blessings, her husband praises her. Many women do noble things, but she does all things without trusting her charm or beauty. She fears the Lord.

Working is part of God's plan for women. We see other women working throughout the Bible. Lydia sold purple dye, Phoebe was a leader and deacon, and Priscilla is often thought of as a tentmaker.[11] Still, Priscilla was many other things in her lifetime: a businesswoman, a refugee, a traveling evangelist, and a church planter.

Priscilla and her husband, Aquila, were what we'd call today a power couple. They were missionaries with Paul and also worked with leather. Priscilla is an equal partner with her husband, reflecting back to Eve's original design. This couple exemplifies the ideal of marriage—two becoming one, functioning as a unit, powerful in ministry.[12]

Shiphrah and Puah were midwives and responsible for saving Moses since Pharaoh had ordered that all Israelite boy babies be killed. Rahab was an innkeeper. Deborah was a prophet, judge, and leader for the Israelites. Hudlah was a prophet and a teacher.[13]

Deborah is the only female judge mentioned in the Bible. So the patriarchy has never been absolute. God has always been affirming His original design in creating women.

Deborah was courageous, serving in a difficult time, leading with knowledge and wisdom. She was trusted. She was confident and direct; she was humble. She inspired the Israelites to victory over their Canaanite oppressors.[14]

GOD HAS CREATED EACH OF US FOR A PURPOSE, AND OUR NUMBER-ONE PRIORITY IS TO LOVE GOD AND DO HIS WILL.

His will for your life is not likely the same as His will is for my life. There is no denying that God has created women to have children and to raise our children. But the majority of women are called to work in and outside the home. A single woman, a divorced woman, a widow, or a woman who works due to financial needs is actually embodying Biblical principles. It is sad and damaging to many women in the modern church that so much emphasis is placed on motherhood and homemaking. Barren women, single women, divorced women, widows, career women...feel marginalized in churches, as if not fulfilling their "womanhood."

If you have struggled with mom guilt, overworking like me, you can put it to rest. If you've experienced shame or guilty from being childlessness or if you choose to remain single and childless in favor of a career, you no longer need to carry this burden. Work is worship.

THE INDUSTRIAL REVOLUTION

Throughout history, a woman's life could be quite different depending on where she lived. Over time, it's been common for rulers to create laws that restrict people's rights for fear they would become too strong and overtake them. Oppression and fear-based leadership have held women back from being who they were intended to be. Looking at the history of oppressed people, a person's wealth always has a considerable influence on opportunities and future outcomes—having money provides the luxury of time and educational resources, which often leads to advancement in the workplace.

In many parts of the world, women were (and still are) considered to be property, not people—meaning they had no rights to their bodies and couldn't own anything because they were property themselves. In the 1800s, the Industrial Revolution caused a significant turning point for women in America. Up until this time, there wasn't a clear segregation of jobs. Women were expected to do hard work and needed to work for their families to survive. Children helped take care of the families' needs, much of the work done in or at home.[15]

During the Industrial Revolution, things changed. With the needs of large manufacturing facilities came new working opportunities. These new jobs had extremely harsh working conditions, especially for women and children. Because of such conditions and the naturally sinful nature of people, laws were created to help protect women and children.

These changes drastically impacted society. Work traditionally done inside the home was now being done in factories, and men were expected to work harder to financially provide for their families' needs. The working conditions were harsh for men, too, and often required fourteen-hour workdays. This resulted in men being seen as the "breadwinner" and changed the family structure where men became more of an authority.[16]

In the nineteenth and twentieth centuries, women started to enter the workforce in roles such as teachers and clerical assistants due to social and economic changes, and employers began to hire women for these roles, knowing that they could pay them less because their husbands were paid more. Single women were compensated at lower rates because they only needed to take care of themselves or work until they found a husband and had a family.[17]

During World War II, women were needed in factories doing

"man's work" not only to provide for their family but for the companies to remain open. During the war, women did a great job, better and more efficient work than men in some areas.[18] Many women were even awarded medals for their work, as it aided greatly in the war efforts.[19]

When the war was over, and the men returned home, it was expected that women would leave their jobs and return to their homes. However, many women enjoyed working and didn't want to return home. If a woman remained working, she was often looked down upon as taking a man's opportunity.[20]

LAWS THAT SUPPORT WOMEN AT WORK

In the sixties and seventies, many gains were made for women in the workforce. In 1963, the Equal Pay Act was passed by Congress with a promise that men and women would be paid an equal wage for performing similar work for jobs that require equal skill, effort, and responsibility. Title VII of the Civil Rights Act of 1964 made it unlawful for employers and employment agencies to fail or refuse to hire or refer—or otherwise to discriminate against—any individual based on race, color, religion, sex, or national origin—including hiring, firing, training, and promotions.

These trends continued from the seventies to the early 2000s. As of June 2021, the Paycheck Fairness Act was passed in the House of Representatives. If passed in the Senate, this act would fill in the loopholes left by the 1963 Equal Pay Act, and women would make many gains to obtain equal pay for equal roles.

While these laws support women's rights, they will do little to close the gap in a woman's position at work. The jobs we hold at work are not likely to ever be entirely fixed by laws, nationally or globally. Experts estimated that it would take 99.5 years to close the gap before the global pandemic of 2020. After the pandemic, it's now estimated that it will take 135.6 years to close the job and pay gap, which can vary based on the country you live in, largely depending on access to education and financial resources.[21] In addition to the violence and abuse women frequently experience at home and in the workforce, women also face challenges of perception set by societal norms that have determined the roles women are expected to perform for generations.

OUR CULTURE'S IMPACT

The way women are portrayed in society and media directly affects what other women view as available to them. In 2019, only fourteen of the top one hundred movies had a balance in speaking roles by gender. For every female with a named speaking role, there are 1.9 males. Women are more likely than men to be shown as parents and have a known marital status. Seventy-three percent of male characters but 61 percent of female characters had an identifiable job or occupation. A larger proportion of male than female characters were seen in their work setting, actually working (59 percent versus 43 percent). Male characters were more likely than females to be seen in primarily work-related roles (60 percent versus 40 percent). Female characters were more likely than males to be seen in mostly personal life-related roles (52 percent versus 34 percent). Females comprised 26 percent of leaders, while males accounted for 74 percent of leaders.[22]

In Hollywood, female actresses peak faster and have fewer opportunities as they age. Women are typically in their prime for roles between the ages of twenty and thirty, where men continue to get cast more into their forties and fifties. Women are often cast in roles that portray them in a sexual manner, an overbearing mother or wife role, or a star man's partner. It seems innocent, but TV, social media, YouTube, and magazines affect who and how women think they are supposed to be.

The media that we surround ourselves with directly affects how we view ourselves in society and what we see as available to us. We need to get back to God's original design and Biblical role models!

Parents' raising their children reflect their views on how and what they think their children should do. From the colors of things, to the books they read, toys they buy, and activities they involve them in. They teach them what they should want in life.

For many women, finding a good man to take care of them is a goal—not a goal that they have set, but a goal that their parents and society set for them years ago. Don't get me wrong, I want my girls to have great relationships and marriages, but I equally want them to achieve their dreams along with those relationships.

When it comes to relationships, we train girls to wait for the boys. We teach our girls to wait to be noticed and validated by others. It's not that parents are intentionally trying to hold their girls back from being all they can be. My mom called herself "old fashioned." When I was in high school, I wanted to go to my sophomore prom, and I found the most beautiful royal blue dress that was whisked back to the store when I wasn't asked by a boy to go to prom. My school was small, and I could have gone as a sophomore without a date.

As parents, we tend to think that our kids will get over it, and

I did. I forgave my mom. It wasn't until she reminded me that her mother wouldn't let her go to prom without a date that I recalled that I couldn't go either. These damaging subliminal messages stay with most of us forever and affect our behavior and perceptions.

Society tells our girls to wait, have good manners, be kind, agreeable, sexy, and if you're good enough, then you will get attention. If you're fortunate, then one day, a man will ask for your hand in marriage. At work, we tend to do the same thing and wait for others to notice us, give us opportunities, and for others to give us our value.

To change future generations of women, we need to change how society portrays women and how we raise our children. The more women are seen in executive and political roles across the world, the younger women will be inspired to see themselves in those roles.

The good news is that God says you are capable of so much more.[23]

We're now we're seeing encouraging trends in the workplace too.

STUDIES SHOW THAT COMPANIES WITH WOMEN COMPRISING 30 PERCENT OR MORE OF EXECUTIVE- AND DIRECTOR-LEVEL LEADERSHIP POSITIONS OUTPERFORM OTHER COMPANIES.

Because it makes good business sense to have women in executive positions, many companies are now moving toward more diverse leadership teams because of these findings.[24] This follows the *ezer kenegdo* design that God has created women with. God not only sees us this way but has provided powerful women examples in the Bible to follow.

So what will it take to increase the number of executive positions filled by women?

As diversity continues to be an essential factor for many companies, they strive to build teams that incorporate men and women. Companies continue to struggle with these initiatives for many reasons, but one of the biggest challenges is having women step up for promotion opportunities. Women tend not to raise their hand for an opening unless they feel 100 percent qualified. Men raise their hands if they meet 60 percent of the qualifications.[25] Like everything else in life, career advancement is a learning process, and the best way to learn is to get experience. If you want to be better at taking the next step in your career, the best thing you can do is ask for the position and start doing it.

I've never been 100 percent ready for any promotion that I've received. There will always be more to learn and ways that I can grow. You can do it too, and it doesn't have to be stressful and complicated like the world leads you to believe. We don't have to look to reality to decide what is possible for us. When we have God in our hearts and follow His plan for our lives, we have access to His wisdom and strength, the same way that Ruth and Esther did. You have the Spirit of God in you, and He wants you to experience Holy Righteousness and abundant joy. Take God's word and break the cultural lies and bounds.

YOU ARE ALREADY ENOUGH: CLAIM YOUR VALUE

All humans have unconscious biases, also known as implicit bias.

An implicit bias is an assumption or judgment that we make automatically, without thinking or conscious thought. Have you ever shifted your purse to the other side of your body when you notice someone walking down the street? I'm not knocking anyone's needs for safety, but this simple act is an example of unconscious bias. You judge the person as unsafe or risky and make an adjustment. You don't know the person, and yet you react because of a belief that you have adopted that this person is potentially unsafe. This doesn't make you a bad person; it makes you human.

At work, implicit bias looks like a male manager not suggesting to a woman (who happens to be a mom) that she should put in for a promotion. Unconsciously, he thinks that the woman wouldn't want to take on a new role.

Implicit bias is a massive contributor to the gender parity gap. Men and women have unconscious biases, but few people know that they do. People, in general, intend to be good people and believe themselves to be good people.

Implicit bias is a silent problem and why women need to advocate for themselves. We can't identify our implicit biases because we don't believe ourselves to be biased. In our minds, we have made logical and rational decisions based on the facts.

There have been countless studies done on implicit biases. The studies find that women are not less intelligent, talented, or hardworking than their male counterparts. As a collective, men and women only perceive women as less intelligent, talented, powerful, and hardworking than men.

One study found that boys outperformed girls on a math test, but when the names were removed from the test, the girls outperformed the boys. All of the teachers grading the test were women.[26] Yes, you read that right, MATH scores!

Other studies show the same pattern. The Hubble telescope is only able to be used by a limited number of people each year. Students write papers to apply to be part of that group. Researchers found that from 2001 to 2012, women's papers were accepted 19 percent on average, and men's proposals were accepted 23 percent on average. Although the gap wasn't large, in 2018, they had anonymous submissions, and for the first time, the women outperformed the men.[27]

Similar studies have been conducted with women's computer code being rejected more than men's. When anonymous submissions of computer code are evaluated, women's code is selected more than the men's code.[28]

The same thing happens when identical resumes are submitted for men and women.[29] Many companies are working to remove the bias by doing blind interviews and removing any information suggesting a person's gender from their resumes.

Implicit bias plays a role in promotions. When men mentor other men, they are more likely to teach them the skills they need to learn, but when men mentor women, they most often focus on their personality or leadership skills.

They say knowledge is power. But knowledge is only one half of the equation. Knowledge without action is frustration. If all we needed was knowledge, then we would all be skinny, rich, and happy. Looking back at history and perceptions of women in the workplace, we can see how implicit bias has hindered the growth of women and of companies as a whole. These biases impact education, job opportunities, promotions, and even interpersonal relations in the workplace. Women are three times more likely to be interrupted in meetings than men; that includes women interrupting women.[30] All people unknowingly experience height bias, fitness bias, beauty bias, and more.

So, this is where we come in. We have to step up to be part of the solution. Once we step up, we have to repeatedly step up and support other women in stepping up too. Implicit and explicit bias are not the only factors in the lack of women's career advancement.

AS WOMEN, WE HAVE TO STOP WAITING FOR OTHERS TO NOTICE US AND START CLAIMING OUR VALUE NOW.

We know that implicit bias could have a negative impact on your advancement because of an underlying belief that women don't want more from their career. So if there is an opening or an opportunity that you want, then you have to make it known. It's time to stop underestimating our value and ability in the workplace, focusing on perceived qualification gaps. Studies show that women will pay themselves less than others for doing the same work, where men will value their work at a higher level.[31]

As a whole, women are vastly undervaluing themselves and are often shocked to hear that such major placement and pay gaps exist. One of the key areas where this problem starts is in salary negotiation. Studies have shown that 57 percent of men negotiate their salaries, whereas only 7 percent of women negotiate. Those who do negotiate are reported to receive salary increases of 7.6 percent.[32] But if women simply aren't negotiating, it sets a lousy precedent that's hard to reverse. These behaviors can be linked back to how girls are raised. Negotiating isn't "nice," isn't demure, and isn't "ladylike."

When I graduated from college, I received three job offers, one of which was from one of the most sought-after companies. It would have been easy for me to ask for more money or more time off, but I didn't. I wasn't scared. It just never occurred to me that I should.

Once I started the job, I quickly learned that others with lesser skills had better salaries than I had. It was frustrating to see others making more, but I didn't understand that it was my responsibility to set my own value from the start. My regional manager even told me that I was the person they wanted to hire and they were thrilled I accepted the offer. So I can see now that I would have probably earned more from day one had I negotiated.

After realizing that others were making more than I was, I took it upon myself to ask for more, and it worked. Once my manager told me, "I'm not sure we can get you to that number," but he did.

Over time this adds up fast. Suppose at age thirty, two equally qualified applicants, Jessica and Elizabeth, get job offers for $100,000 a year. Elizabeth negotiates and receives $107,600, while Jessica accepts the original $100,000, grateful for the opportunity. Year after year, they both receive the same 3 per cent pay raises. In the first year, Elizabeth earns an additional $7,600. By age sixty-five, Elizabeth will earn $3,489,193 more than Jessica in salary alone.

We wait to be confident, educated, and have the know-how to be successful in a role before raising our hands.

Today, women make just over 50 percent of the workforce.[33] We have to stop waiting to be perfect, waiting for someone else to pick us, waiting for someone else to value us, or waiting for the perfect time.

CHAPTER 3

FLOWING OVER STRIVING

For me, career advancement was something that you are supposed to do. After graduating from college and landing a job, the only thing left to do was climb the corporate ladder. After all, this is what it takes to be a successful and responsible part of society. Right?

In less than two years after graduating, I was promoted to kitchen manager. My first taste of success was exhilarating. I was willing to work long hours, absorb the stress, and would take on any obstacle that was in my way. But inside I felt empty and longed to be loved. I tried to fill the void with men, alcohol, and achievements. But I was never whole. My career became my identity and the place I felt valued. This was the start of a path that would lead me to strive for success.

Women in the workforce have different desires when it comes to career advancement. Some women are shooting for the top spot, some are ok with whatever is given to them, others are content with their current role. Some women work part-time for a convenient job, and others feel it's not worth working with the cost of childcare.

Each of us is afforded a finite number of hours on Earth, and what we do with those hours matters more than you think. Jobs in our society have been depicted as chores that steal our lives, but this is not how God intended for us to live and view our work. By design, work is worship. Work as unto the Lord.[34]

The problem is most people are continually striving in their jobs and life rather than flowing.

To understand what I mean by flowing, think of Cinderella, a woman who lived in flow surrounded by stepsisters who were always striving. In the classic Disney movie, we see Cinderella cooking, cleaning, and being treated awfully by her own family. Despite her circumstances, Cinderella doesn't focus on the despair that many would call her current reality. Instead, she serves her family, cares for the animals, sings, dances, and hopes for the future. When faced with a challenge of not having a dress for the ball, we see her rewarded by friends, the birds and mice, who rally around her to make a beautiful gown. Cinderella graciously accepts help and doesn't think less of herself because of it.

Comparatively, her stepsisters are always striving with a selfish attitude, and no matter what is done for them, they're never satisfied. They steal and destroy Cinderella's dress because they believe that only one of them can succeed in winning the prince's hand. They are seated in the place of honor, and yet their hearts are filled with envy and anger.

When the glass slipper is found, each of the stepsisters insists that it's hers and crams and shoves her foot in, trying to make something fit that clearly doesn't. When it's Cinderella's turn, her foot glides into the glass slipper with a comfortable flow, and she is whisked off to the castle to live happily ever after with the prince.

As a child, this movie's theme was all about meeting Prince Charming and living a perfect life—what a fairy tale. From a career perspective, it offers a recipe for a peaceful life of abundance.

Cinderella models what it means to flow. To flow is to live without anxiety for the future or worries of the past. When we flow in life, we are not forcing things to happen, but enjoying what's in front of us now. We take the first step toward a goal without knowing what each step will be. Although we may have a destination in mind, we don't force the issue. We enjoy each step of the journey. To flow is to be at peace, and this peaceful outlook allows us to have a clear mind and more readily take the next step required to realize our purpose. Flowing doesn't fixate on failure but sees each failure as a gift to learn from. To flow is to dream and believe that those dreams will come true. When in flow, we humbly seek and accept help.

Striving, on the other hand, produces a life of stress, frustration, anger, envy, pride, and worry. It races for the finish line looking for success and won't take a moment to rest. Striving overthinks the actions of others and believes that the ends justify the means, no matter who gets hurt along the way. Most often, striving keeps us up at night because it reminds us what we lack or that we have failed or cannot do what we have set out to do. Striving hardens our hearts with pride, leaving us unable to seek guidance or help from others.

Striving says that if everything isn't perfect, I have failed, and I must try harder. Striving causes fear, and where there is fear, there cannot be love. God has not given us a spirit of fear, and His yoke is easy.[35] When we strive in life, we put stress on our physical health, mental health, families, careers, and relationships. Often, we don't realize that we are striving in life or that striving in life is even a bad thing because no one has taught us to flow. Although we may not identify ourselves with striving, we feel its effects in every aspect of life.

Striving happens for different reasons for different people. When we focus on things that we are supposed to do and should be doing, we get easily dragged into a world where striving is the only way to meet society's demands. Society shapes our worldview and tells us where we should be, what we should have, and what success is. We use social media, TV shows, magazines, commercials, and the Joneses next door to determine our success level in today's world.

Depending on how long we have been striving and what we are striving for, our worldview changes—creating limiting beliefs deep within us without even realizing what is happening. These limiting beliefs hold us back from even trying things or hoping for a future that we cannot plan every step of the way. You give up on the dreams of the past and you minimize your future by only hoping for what you already know you can realistically achieve. You settle and remain stuck.

Flowing is about confidently taking each step without hesitation or reservation. To flow is to embrace learning new skills, and trying new things, without knowing the outcome until the next step is taken. Flow is patient and at peace in times of uncertainty.

In your career, flowing is taking on the next project, helping others, and being the best you can be because you care about the company's mission and people. It's doing work that you love and taking chances to try something new. It's believing in yourself and enjoying each step of the journey. To flow operates from a place of hope, not only optimism. Hope takes action in faith when optimism doesn't require action, only a positive outlook. When we are in flow, we are bold, brave, and courageous.

When we are flowing in our lives and careers, we believe in our dreams. No matter how far-fetched they are to the outside world, we internally know that God gives us the desires of our hearts when our hope is focused on Him—and when our heart and its desires are in alignment with His.[36] We operate in faith, and when we face adversity, we remain hopeful and joyful, knowing that the Lord is our Provider, our Healer, our Deliverer, and our Source of life. We turn to prayer and continue to worship God in all circumstances.

When we are flowing, we can think clearly and fill our heads with positive thoughts for the future. We know without a doubt that God is with us and going before us to make a way to deliver a better and brighter future. We stay focused on the work that the Lord has called and created us to—without fear. Our words, thoughts, motives, and actions are in harmony.

An amazing example of flowing in the Bible is found in the Acts of the Apostles, Chapter 16, when Paul was on his second missionary journey. During this journey, Paul and Silas run into a slave girl while going to pray. They help deliver her from the trapped spirit inside her that earned her masters a lot of money by fortune-telling. The masters are so upset because of what Paul and Silas had done that they start riots and have the disciples of

Jesus thrown into jail. They are put into the inner dungeon, and their feet are clamped to the stocks.

That night around midnight, Paul and Silas are praying to God and singing hymns. They are clearly focused on one thing: doing the will of God. It would have been easy and acceptable by worldly standards for Paul and Silas to be afraid, angry, hostile, and frustrated. But they weren't. In true flow fashion, they gave thanks to the Lord and remained faithful in their pursuit to do the will of the Lord.

As the two men worshiped God, an earthquake happened—and all the doors immediately flew open, and the chains of every prisoner fell off. Paul remained in the cell when he saw that the jailer was going to kill himself after seeing what had happened on his watch. Paul stopped him, explained that he and the others weren't leaving, and the grateful jailer accepted Christ. Paul and Silas were focused on their goal even when their reality was painting a much different picture.

In the Bible, we also see examples of people striving when God has already given them a promise. In the case of Abraham and Sarah, they determine that they are too old to have children, and instead of trusting God and living in flow, they take it into their own hands by having Sarah's servant sleep with Abraham. The striving to accomplish the goal fell short of what God intended. Once again, God told Abraham that Sarah would have a son, and this time their flowing with God's promise led to Sarah becoming pregnant.[37]

The story of Jacob in the Bible is another great illustration of a life of striving.[38]

When Esau and Jacob were born, God spoke to Rebekah and

told her that her older son would serve her younger son. Early on, Esau sold his birthright to Jacob for a bowl of stew. When Isaac grew older, he told Esau to go out to hunt him some game, prepare it for him, and then he would give Esau his blessing as the firstborn. Instead of talking to Isaac or turning to God for help, Rebekah overheard this and took matters into her own hands, telling Jacob to gather a couple of goats that she would prepare. He followed her plan, put on Esau's clothes, and wore goat skin to mimic the hair of his brother's skin.

When he presented the offering to his father, he lied to his father several times, claiming he was in fact his brother. When his brother, Esau, arrived home and found out what happened, he was furious. Esau plotted to kill Jacob. When we strive in our lives and careers, we miss the best that God has planned for us.

A career in flow doesn't concern itself with what reality says is possible. It keeps its eyes locked on the Lord, working willingly and following the voice of God. Many times in my career, I could hear God telling me that I needed to take a different step. These steps were not "realistic or practical." Once I gave away everything I owned and moved across the country to a city where I had no job. Another time I took a job making less than I had when I graduated from college. I knew that God was calling me to these places because, although reality wasn't on my side, there was a peace that surpasses all understanding in my heart.[39]

WHEN GOD SPEAKS TO US, WE HAVE A CHOICE IN OUR ACTIONS.

When we live in flow, we accept Holy Righteousness and follow God's laws out of love, not obligation. God has already given us everything, so there is no need to earn anything. We work hard, remain humble, love others, and seek wisdom. We take action with integrity, not worrying about what the world around us says about our odds. We believe that God is with us and has already gone before us to make a path.

As humans, we're all created to contribute to the greater good of the universe. We were not merely put on this Earth to consume and to strive. Career advancement has gotten a bad reputation for being more about striving for position, power, and money. It can be, and those who seek positions, power, and money will get those things along with loads of stress, fear, anxiety, and worry.

Being ambitious is not a bad thing. Ambition is God-given and is about performing at your highest potential to make the most of what God has entrusted you with.[40] Why would we not want to glorify God by living an abundant life in service to him? He created us to be courageous servant leaders and disciples.

Most often, Christians are led to believe that money is the root of all evil and that they shouldn't have things because it's better to give than receive.[41] God wants you to have money. In fact, He knows that you need to have money to live. So how much money is too much money? The amount of money that takes your trust off the Lord. It could be one hundred dollars, or it could be one hundred million dollars. Money itself isn't evil. The Bible says that it's loving and trusting money as your God that is the root of all evil.

When God tells us that it is more blessed to give than receive, it's a factual statement.[42]

Your body chemistry changes when you give, and your happiness increases. Generosity and giving are part of being a good steward.

When we make more money, we can give more money. My hope for you is to have enough money to fulfill any need that God would place on your heart. No matter our current income, we should be giving joyfully now. How much should we give? The amount you give isn't as important as the motive and emotion in your heart toward giving. God isn't going to love you any more or any less because of what you give. But generosity is a Kingdom principle, and if you're not currently giving, then I encourage you to talk to God and see where He wants you to give now. This isn't about tithing your way to wealth; it's about listening to God and being a good steward of the resources He has given you to manage.[43]

God created us to live abundantly. Jesus worked, and Jesus accepted money from others to do His ministry. Paying fair wages is mentioned in the Bible countless times, and Solomon is known as the richest man who ever lived.[44] Money is a tool and a means to advance the will of God. To want more money doesn't make you a bad person or less of a Christian. What God tells us is that money should not be where our safety and security come from. We shouldn't idolize money or make our worship dependent upon things. Money shouldn't stop us from living out God's will with faith, and we should earn our money fairly. When we are living in flow, money is not why we do what we do, and we willingly give generously to others. In flow, our first and primary focus is the Lord.

When striving, ambition and money take on a different role. Ambition in strive mode is filled with pride, manipulation, schemes, selfishness, and sin. When striving, we don't care who we hurt or the welfare of others as long as we continue to receive more. Money is our security blanket, and no matter how much money we have, we are always aware of those that have more.

Striving holds tightly to money, for if it were to let go, then life wouldn't be worth living. Striving believes that happiness and joy come from a plump bank account and material things. You could be the richest woman in the world, and you still wouldn't be happy.

People claim that they do not want to be an executive because they believe that position, power, and money are unnecessary. That's because society paints position, power, and money as bad things. The truth is that Jesus had position, power, and money, and He used these things to do the will of God. Jesus never allowed those things to be His identity, and He used them for good. In many cases, people who do not wish to advance their careers lack the desire because they once had a manager who took advantage of their position or was a jerk. Possibly, they have repeatedly heard how hard and demanding it is to lead from the top.

To be clear, leading in an executive position is not a walk in the park, and there are many skills that you have to obtain to be a successful leader. As my mentor and friend John Maxwell says, "There are no two consecutive good days in a leader's life." Being an executive is not a pass to freedom. It's sure to provide you with challenges—challenges that you currently can't imagine being able to overcome. Being an executive or having an executive title is not the ultimate goal of career advancement.

THE GOAL IS LIVING OUT YOUR GOD-GIVEN AMBITION AS AN ACT OF WORSHIP TO ADVANCE THE KINGDOM THAT HE HAS CREATED.

Maybe you don't desire to be an executive; that's ok. We are all uniquely gifted and created for a purpose. Yet, many people will never reach their full potential because they settle for what they can see right in front of them that appears to be safe and secure. When our goal is safety and security, then we limit ourselves to our capabilities at this moment. God created us to have fulfilling lives and teaches us in the Bible to work as if we are working for the Lord and not men.[45] When we are flowing in our careers, we work joyfully and take risks. When we are striving, we remain stuck where we were never intended to be. You were born to live a life of flow where your dreams become a reality and peace is your default state.

DREAM BIG

In order for us to accomplish our dreams, we first must dream. Growing up, my family lacked financial security. However, I was never so poor that I starved or didn't have secondhand clothes. I knew that we weren't the worst off because we would spend time working at the soup kitchen to feed the homeless. My parents worked hard—both of them, and sometimes multiple jobs.

I love my parents deeply, and I'm grateful for the many things they taught me.

Their hard work couldn't change how I felt—for me being poor caused a lot of insecurity, starting in grade school. I was one of those kids that had a heightened awareness of all of the things that I lacked. As a kid, I would daydream a lot. I remember sitting in class and staring out the window, watching the leaves swaying and twirling in the wind as I let my mind wander. I would dream of all sorts of things—from the way I wanted to decorate my bedroom, to how life would be when I was an adult, to the boy that I wanted to secretly date. These dreams were alive, and I can still remember the warm feeling in my body as I envisioned my future. Then as I grew older and started to understand how the world works, I stopped dreaming about what was possible and started to focus on what was probable.

As children, we are taught to dream and imagine what we want to be when we grow up. The most common things girls want to be are teachers, veterinarians, and doctors. For boys, it's professional athletes, musicians, and doctors. For me, I always wanted to be a mom of five with a handsome husband who coached sports. Nearly one-third of the time, people achieve their childhood career goals.[46] I'm getting close with four children and a handsome husband who coaches.

When we look at why kids choose these professions, it's primarily based on the interactions and feelings that kids have toward people in these roles. Still, more than anything else today, kids base their choices on media influences like TV and YouTube. Researchers have also found that you may have a different affinity to acquire specific careers based on where you grow up. While doctors tend to outweigh all other professional desires, each region has a secondary underlying career choice. Living in Texas makes you more likely to want to be an engineer, while living in the West makes more kids desire to become astronauts.[47] A child's gender also plays a large role in the type of career they will desire.

When we look at this seemingly fun and exciting exercise of kids establishing their future ambitions, we don't think of it as anything more than a cute homework assignment.

One-third of children reach their career goals, leaving two-thirds not reaching their early career goals. This is a good thing. If everyone were doctors, vets, athletes, musicians, and teachers, there would be a lot of work left undone. But you have to ask the question, why is it that some reach their goals while others don't?

The way that others react to our dreams has a significant impact on the success of those goals. When I was in high school, I didn't view myself as intelligent. My mom had preached going to college our entire lives. It didn't appear that there was another option. Still, as a senior, I wasn't going to apply to colleges because I didn't believe that I could get in. I decided to be a masseuse because I was good at giving massages. Nothing against masseuses; I'm grateful for your gifts and the way you relax my body. More than the profession, the point I'm making is that I didn't believe in myself enough to go to college. Others kind of agreed with me by helping to get the massage school applications ready. That was until I took a trip to Las Vegas with the family I babysat for. I grew up in a small country town and had never seen anything like it before.

I don't know if it was the lights, glitz, or glam, but when I came home, I wanted to run a large hotel in Las Vegas. When I told my mother, the first thing she did was pick up the phone to call the Hilton in Pittsburgh, Pennsylvania, to ask them where I should go to school.

Because my mom took a supportive role with my dream, it moved forward, and I graduated from Penn State. Suppose my mom would have told me, "Mary, that's a crazy idea," or, "Mary, you're not smart enough," or, "Mary, where will we get the money to send you to school?" or, "Mary, you already did the work to go to another school. You should do that." Then my chances of obtaining my dream job would have been greatly diminished.

Well-meaning parents and some outright mean parents have diminished and destroyed many dreams. After deciding what they want to do when they grow up, some students are met with laughs, we can't afford it, get another dream, or who do you know from here that has ever done that? Or a parent that only sees their child's current abilities, and because they are not ready for that career now tries to protect them by "being real" with them to spare them from crushed dreams. Or a parent who, out of all good intentions, started to guide their child toward something more reasonable, in the family business or a career with a higher income.

Suppose a parent, teacher, family member, or friend doesn't crush their dreams. In that case, by the end of middle school, many start to set their boundaries in life based on their perception of what they are capable of—factoring in grades, class rank, and economic status.

When children are supported emotionally in the home, and their parents encourage them toward their goals, they are more likely to succeed. It doesn't mean that you are doomed if you didn't hit the parent jackpot, and if you're like me, and reading this as a parent and feel like you have possibly limited your child's future, there is hope.

Parents or guardians play the most prominent role only because they typically spend the most time with their children. Other influences can and do impact children in a big way. It could be a teacher, family member, friend, mentor, someone you happen to meet by chance, even a book or video. When another person takes the time to invest even a single word of encouragement, it can change a person's life. We will get into more about how this happens in the upcoming chapters. But in a moment, like when I went to Vegas, a person's mind can be activated toward believing they can achieve their dreams.

Sadly many people will never encounter this positive word of encouragement that unleashes their potential. All of our words make a difference, and I encourage you to point out and lift both children and adults, especially those that others might overlook. You never know: you might be their Vegas—or in Cinderella's case, the birds, mice, and Fairy Godmother.

Because of our backgrounds and upbringing, we have a unique perspective on the importance of advancing our careers and what it represents. When I struggled to understand how to advance in my career, I couldn't see my abilities or value.

My husband and I would have daily conversations about my ability to be an executive. Each day he would tell me how capable I was and why I was perfect for the role, and I would point out every flaw that I had. Even the most superficial flaw was a reason for me not to believe that I was capable of more.

Looking back, I can see how crazy I must have sounded. I was facing a major case of imposter syndrome. Imposter syndrome is when we feel less than, and we are waiting for everyone else to figure it out. When you are in the middle of imposter syndrome, it's hard to realize that everyone else has felt this way—from movie stars to models to CEOs—everyone gets these feelings sometimes. They simply are not true.

In my case, I was recently named team member of the year, I was previously a manager and led large teams, I had the largest and most successful load of coaching clients, I had been chosen time after time for past promotions and new job opportunities.

I don't share this to impress you, but to impress upon you that we are often more ready and capable to advance than we think.

I didn't know that many women were having the same struggles until I started sharing my story, and every time, I heard, "That's my girlfriend," or, "That's my wife," or, "That's me."

ONE OF THE BEST WAYS TO OVERCOME A SITUATION IS TO UNDERSTAND WHAT'S HAPPENING. WHEN WE HAVE THE KNOWLEDGE, WE HAVE A NEW OPPORTUNITY TO ACT ACCORDINGLY, AND THAT'S POWER.

Women throughout history have faced many challenges in the workplace. Countless studies have been conducted and are being conducted to figure out why women are making less than men for the same work—and why so few women are filling seats at the executive tables. Some great books and articles have been written that dive deeper into women's history and the primary problems.

The reasons vary from study to study. Some think it's that women don't ask for a raise or promotion, others believe that women ask just as much but don't get it, others think it's the way that women ask, others think it's because women have so much to do at home, others don't think women should work at all, and the smaller majority believe that women are less valuable than men in the workplace. Women have been said to have a more fixed mindset, meaning that they only view what's possible based on what they have been told.

When polled, women will openly share that they don't pursue career advancement or increased compensation because they fear their manager will fire them, or it will ruin their relationship with their manager.[48] Women valued others above themselves even though they said they worked harder. Women don't know how or like to negotiate and often don't know what value they should place on themselves.[49]

Some women will say that they don't want to advance, others don't know how to advance, and still, others allow their past to limit their future.

I believe that it's all of the above; as humans, we don't all think and act the same way. Sure, one poll might be right—maybe women do ask just as much as men—but that might not be you. Once my manager told me to put an ad out to hire a manager. It never occurred to me that I should have said I would be the manager. I was a successful manager before switching career fields. I'd never been his manager, but the fact that he didn't ask me to be, I felt I wasn't the right one.

Or maybe you have asked and not gotten what you wanted and now feel defeated. I've been there too. I was once told that I would have a salary review in six months. After asking repeatedly and chasing people around the office, it didn't come for an additional nine months. I wasn't given the amount I wanted, but I didn't say anything because I didn't know that I should. That was a stressful time for me, and it made me question my value.

No matter your reason for not getting a raise or promotion, the tools and the My Promotion Plan blueprint are the answer you have been looking for. There is hope for you; no matter what, everyone reading this book can reach a higher potential and level than you are right now.

Before we build the promotion plan, we need to restore your

courage so you can feel like the powerful and successful person that you were born to be. More courage will lead to more success. Whatever you dream, you will have the tools and knowledge to achieve it.

I've seen the My Promotion Plan process transform the lives of women and not only in their careers but also in their confidence. Our minds are a brilliant tool. We are all capable of learning, changing, and stepping into a life that we love. All that is required is to leave your bags at the door and to take the next step.

Part 2

HARMONIZING YOUR HEART AND RENEWING YOUR MIND

In Part 1, A Woman's Place, we talked about God's plan for women in the workforce, the many challenges that women face even today, the difference between flowing and striving in our careers, and the importance of dreaming.

Before we move into Part 2, we need to address promotion coming from God. Because lasting promotion ultimately comes from the Lord.[50] It can be confusing to figure out what our role is and how God is promoting us. First of all, you are a co-creator with God. He absolutely can make miracles happen, and the reality of your situation is not a factor when God is at work. He can open doors for you that no one else can, and He can also shut doors that no one else can open.[51]

Promotion isn't just about our careers. We are promoted to be wives and mothers. We can be promoted in the community, at church, with the government, or through volunteer work.

THE KEY IS TO HAVE OUR HEARTS CONNECTED TO GOD SO THAT OUR MOTIVES STAY PURE AND OUR DESIRES AT WORK NEVER BECOME IDOLS.

A position at work, wifehood, or motherhood, although not bad things, cannot be our identity or our source of trust. We cannot work to please men alone. God calls us to work as if we were working for Him and not for man.[52]

If our titles become our identity, we become less valuable when stripped away and may face depression. Our titles are just a way to identify us in an organization and not the heart's identity; no matter what happens in our career, we are to remain faithful and full of joy even in our troubles.

Many times, before the promotion comes, we will go through trials. The trials are the waiting period that helps us grow needed skills and perspective to grow our faith for the more significant challenges that lie ahead.

God always wants us to advance. Sometimes we lose sight of that, and when in a desert moment, our faith weakens. It's important to remember that since God is in charge of promotion, you are ready enough when He calls. It doesn't matter what others say around you or if you feel qualified. God qualifies you and gives you gifts from the Holy Spirit to help you.[53]

If we want God to promote us, we need to have a humble heart for the Lord—like Abraham, Ruth, Mary, Joseph, Job, David, and so many more. They weren't perfect, but they loved God, remained faithful, served others, humbled themselves, and asked for God's help. They recognized that God was the provider of everything in their lives, and they waited for the Lord's timing.

When we focus on our relationship with Christ, then God can add everything to us as we come to Him as a servant with a humble, gracious, and faithful heart.

For some of you, it will be a raise before your plan is even completed, for others a promotion, for others a new career path, and for others, God may be promoting you to own your own business. Only you and God can know the path that He wants you on.

When we remember that promotion comes from the Lord, we need not be concerned with the outcomes. Our job isn't to have it all figured out. Our job is to work hard, pray for God's will to be done, surrender to the Lord's will, ask God for what you want, have faith, make a plan, and take action in faith—all while giving the credit to God and, no matter what, remaining humble, hopeful, and joyful in the waiting.[54]

Promotion can come from man too, but that's not what you're seeking. You're not seeking to manipulate, flirt, flatter, scheme, slander, desire more money to place your trust in it, power over others, or win at any cost because *that* type of promotion isn't from God. Although you can do those and get promoted, it's not going to bring you a life of abundance.

Instead, your promotion will come from the Lord, and since it's from the Lord, you will not be prideful in your accomplishments boasting to others, but rather giving all of the thanks and glory to the One that made you and gave you all of your abilities to do an incredible job at work.

In Part 2, we will shift gears as we study how God created our minds and the world. God created the world to be Heaven on Earth; and even though the Fall changed the world, it never changed God's desire for us to live in a continual loving relationship with Him. Yet, many devout Christians are not experiencing a life of peace the way that God has designed it. In this section, you will learn how the hard wiring in your brain and body work along with the unseen laws that God created and Jesus modeled for us to live an abundant life of peace, allowing your heart and mind to prepare for God to promote you.

Actions Taken in Faith is a section I'm introducing to encourage you to set yourself up for success by creating a private sacred place where you can read, journal, pray, and experience all that God has for you. To get the most out of these, get up an hour earlier and complete them at the start of your day. Of course, if you already get up at four in the morning or have a newborn baby, then I'm not recommending that you need to be crazy. In that case, find one hour that works for you to experience all that God has for you. If you can't get an hour, then start with thirty minutes. The key is to be as consistent as possible to reduce the length of time it takes to harmonize your heart and renew your mind. There is no need to beat yourself up if you miss a day. Just get back to it the next day.

Each of us sees the world through a different perspective or lens. Our perspective is created by the experiences that we have had in the world. Our experiences create our personal truths and tell us what is and isn't possible. The problem is our lenses are often cloudy or broken due to past mistakes or past hurts that we are still holding as truths in our minds today. Our perception becomes our reality even when it's not the truth. Have you ever had someone get mad at you and make claims about your actions without confronting you? I know I have, and I've made judgments too.

When we make judgments, they are based on our perspective, which does not necessarily correspond to the other person's true intention. If we are to dream bigger in our lives and careers, then we have to become aware of the lens and challenge its truths. God wants more for your life than you can currently imagine, but in order to experience His abundance, you must desire and believe that it's possible for you. And right now, you might still be having thoughts of doubt run through your mind. You might be thinking, *Sure, this works for others, but I doubt this will work for me* (insert any doubt floating through your mind). It doesn't have to be this way; God's not done with you.

Let's get started on activating the promises of God to create a life of abundance.

CHAPTER 4

UNDERSTANDING OUR MINDS

THE SUBCONSCIOUS MIND

When we think of our mind, we most often think of our brain. But our brain is not our mind—the same way that a musical instrument is not music and a computer is just a large paperweight without software and processing inputs. Our brain is the hardware, in this case, and our subconscious mind is the software. The inputs are our unique experiences, perceptions, and conscious thoughts.

Just as a computer has programs to run the applications on your computer, similarly, your mind has programs that tell your body how to run. The subconscious stores all of the information necessary to breathe, digest food, and pump your heart. It is incredibly efficient, allowing us not to have to think about how to operate our bodies and store what we have learned. It stores everything that you have seen, heard, experienced, and felt since the moment you were conceived. It is a database of every memory, thought, and feeling that operates 95 percent of your life on autopilot. Rather than consciously thinking about each step of an activity you pull from the subconscious mind, it's quite convenient not to have to learn how to walk, talk, or drive every day.

The subconscious mind consists of programs designed to keep you safe and tell you how to feel about different situations. The subconscious is a beautiful thing. But it's not impervious to faulty programming that holds us back or limits us from reaching our highest potential.

It's why behavior modification alone doesn't work. The majority of the subconscious mind is formed from conception through age seven; then, your brain goes through a range of cycles, but it's the theta brainwaves that are especially receptive to external programming.

HOW YOU PERCEIVE LIFE AND WHAT YOU BELIEVE IS POSSIBLE IS A RESULT OF THE SUBCONSCIOUS MIND.

As we grow, that programming develops the equivalent of an autopilot, keeping us safe from touching a hot stove and other possible dangers to our well-being.

The brain has multiple functions that naturally inform our pain and our joy, our waking and sleeping, our restoration and rejuvenation. The problem is that for all the good programming our subconscious provides, it can also store and repeat negative information and patterns. Once a program has been stored, positive or negative, it gets stronger each time it's activated.

Hypnosis has generally not been accepted by Christians because it appears to be some type of voodoo magic mind control.

That's not the case. Hypnosis is when your brain is in the theta brainwave and is more susceptible to enter the subconscious mind, allowing you to program or reprogram the mind with new information.

All of us have been hypnotized unknowingly. The first seven years of our lives are spent in hypnosis, the theta brainwave state.

The brain has five different types of brainwaves: delta, alpha, theta, beta, and gamma. Each day your brain goes through all the first four stages of brainwaves naturally. The delta waves have the lowest frequencies. You most commonly enter the delta stage when you are in deep sleep. This brainwave state is restorative and rejuvenating. When you were born, you were in delta most of the time for the first two years of life. This is why you slept so much.[55]

At the age of two, you started to also go into the theta state. In this state, you are creative, relaxed, and in free flow. This is why children can turn mud and grass into culinary treasures. The frequencies in this state are higher than delta but still relatively slow. After the age of seven, the subconscious mind is still creating programs, although it's harder because now our programs are "hard wired." To access the control panel hypnosis, repetition, or a deeply emotional experience, is required to override the original program.[56]

At the age of seven, the hypnosis ends when we start to have alpha waves. In the alpha state, the frequency of the brainwaves is once again increased. When in the alpha state, you are in a relaxed learning state.[57] Today you enter the alpha state when you take a moment to relax after working on a project, when you wake up, and just before drifting off to bed. In the alpha state, you are in a calm consciousness. At this point, your mind counts on the subconscious programs that it has previously created to help you navigate the world.

At the age of twelve, you start to have beta brainwaves with an even higher frequency. Beta brainwaves are associated with normal waking consciousness and a heightened state of alertness, logic, and critical reasoning—along with stress, anxiety, restlessness, and the nagging inner chatterbox. The majority of adults primarily operate at high beta during their waking hours.[58] It is little wonder that stress is today's most common health problem. At this point, we begin experiencing the pains of adult life. We're increasing our capacity for reason and discernment. We also see an increase in our ability to concentrate, recall, and experience the full range of human satisfaction, or blessing.

Gamma is the highest level of brainwaves. When you are in the gamma state, you are deeply focused. This is a feeling of being "in the zone." When in this state, you have the highest concentration levels and can easily recall information.[59] Although most of us enter gamma without trying, we won't naturally stay in this state of mind. The use of binaural beats and deep meditations can help you enter more easily into the gamma state.[60]

Human Brain Waves by Age

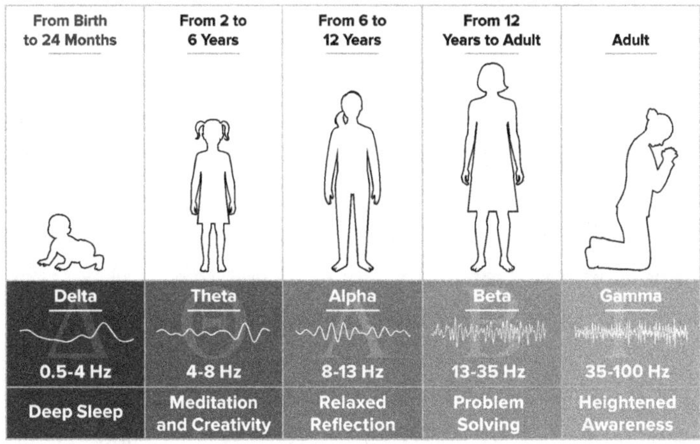

Having a basic understanding of the brainwaves and their function helps us understand why we do, think, and act the way we do each day.

When you consider how the subconscious mind takes shape early in life and develops as we grow, you can start to see why you take on the habits of your mother, no matter how desperately you try not to. We also know that our DNA is passed on to us genetically. So we're now learning how subconscious programs can be passed from generation to generation without anyone knowing it.

A study was done on mice where male mice were shown cherry blossoms, and when they were, they received a mild shock on their foot. They later bred the mice, and the offspring had elevated levels of fear and worry when they smelled cherry blossoms. These mice had never been shocked, and they had never seen their fathers being shocked.[61]

For human beings, this causes problems because we suffer the pain of past generations over and over again. Can you imagine if you and your friends were all smelling cherry blossoms, and because of something that happened to your father, you felt fear and worry? You wouldn't know what caused the fear. Your friends would tell you to get over it or call you weird. But the fear that you are feeling is real. In many ways, this can explain why once a family is on welfare for four generations, it is nearly impossible for anyone within those families to escape those conditions—because the subconscious mind is highly dependent on one's upbringing and environment. This explains why subconscious programming that comes from negative bias against race, gender, and social, economic classes can be so long-lasting and harmful.

Scientists are now discovering that we have the ability to change the expressions of our genes—that we can, in fact, turn them on and off (epigenetics).[62] To consciously change the programming of our genes, we must first have an awareness that we can. If we believe that we will have diabetes because it runs in our family, then we will activate the genes associated with diabetes.

HOW THE SUBCONSCIOUS AND CONSCIOUS MIND WORK TOGETHER

The conscious mind, on the other hand, runs only 5 percent of the time. Each day we have over sixty thousand thoughts. These are the thoughts that we're aware of right now. The conscious mind, unlike the unconscious, is used to process new information and puzzles. Learning and reasoning are first done in the conscious mind. For example, the first time you learned to type on a keyboard, you were using your conscious mind. You had to look down at the keys and think about each key that you wanted to hit. Today, after learning to type, you merely think of the words that you want to appear on the screen, and the fingers go to work, hammering them out with the keys. Today you are pulling from your subconscious mind, where years ago, you learned consciously.

Our conscious mind allows us to think about new things and is a processing center for incoming information.

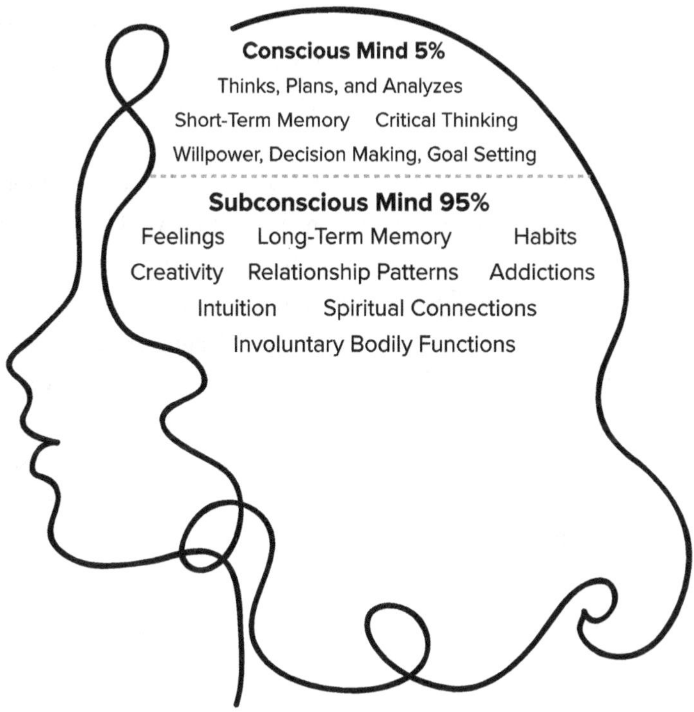

Together the subconscious mind and conscious mind are responsible for our feelings and emotions. Feelings are a product of the subconscious mind and can occur without us trying or understanding why. Emotions are formed in the conscious mind; therefore, we can have control over our emotions.

In the workplace, these parts of our mind are activated in different ways for different reasons.

Say a coworker calls off and leaves you with all of their work to do for the day. The first time that it happens, it might not bother you at all. Then they call off, again and again, requiring you to work longer and harder. The emotions that you are having become stored in your subconscious mind as feelings. Before long, just thinking about your coworker's behavior can lead to immediate feelings of frustration, resentment, and anger—all without a conscious thought. Possibly you believe that this person is taking advantage of you.

Now that we understand that the subconscious mind is running the majority of our lives based on things that we believed by the age of seven, we can now work to identify what we believe to be true. Once we can understand our truth, we can begin to open our mind and ask questions that challenge our beliefs. We can, in fact, change our beliefs, but first, we have to identify the core beliefs before we can rewrite the programming. When you can identify your core beliefs and start to consciously examine each belief, you will gain new understanding and start to renew your mind. By understanding the operating system, you will gain confidence as you learn to manage your thoughts and feelings during your professional growth.

Your Identity is stored in your heart

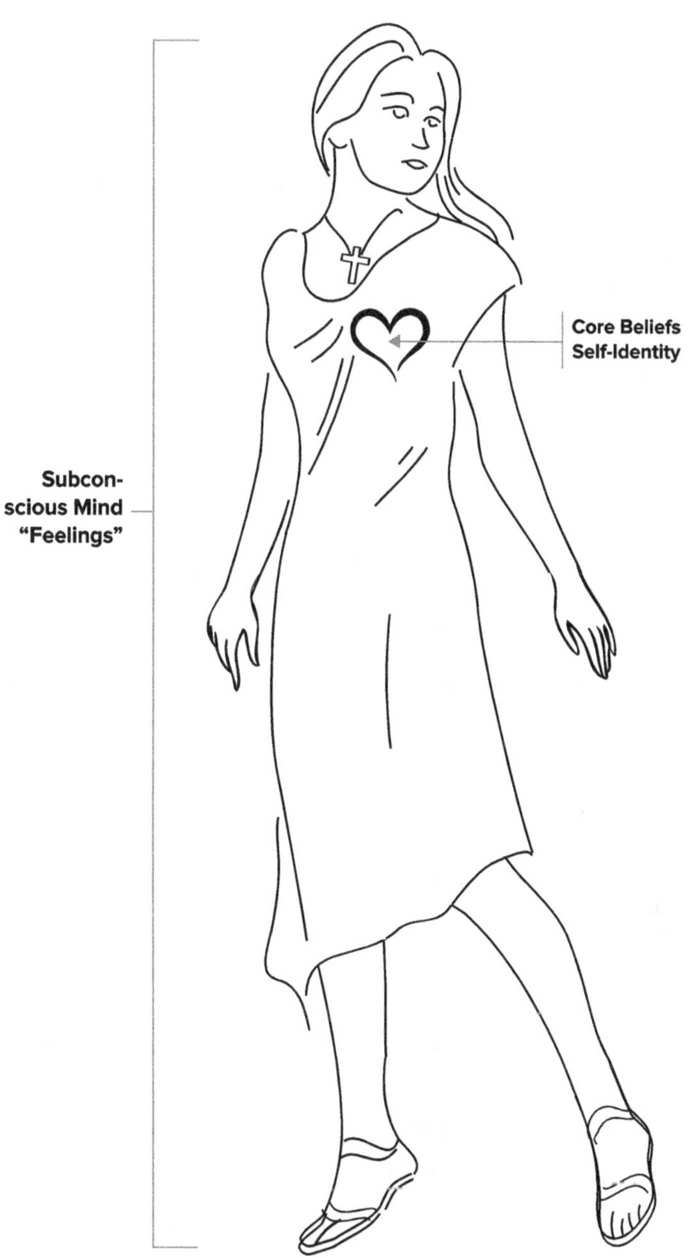

ACTIONS TAKEN IN FAITH

Examine the following list of core beliefs. For each belief, ask yourself if you find the belief to be true or false.

1. I am unlovable.
2. My past failures are holding me back in my ability to advance my career.
3. Making money is hard for me.
4. In order to have a successful career, my family must suffer.
5. I have to be good for God to love me.
6. Others are smarter than I am.
7. Others are more deserving than I am.
8. If I am successful, then I am bad.
9. More success at work will equate to more stress.
10. I have the capacity to advance my career.
11. I am capable of learning new things.
12. I am confident in my ability to prosper.
13. I must do something to be worthy of love.
14. If I am bad, then God won't love me.
15. God wants me to prosper.
16. I am a good steward of the money God has given me.
17. I am confident in my ability to advance my career.
18. I deserve financial abundance.
19. I have released all the guilt from the past that hinders my prosperity.
20. I believe that money is good and that when I have money, I can do good things.
21. I believe that women should work.
22. I believe that I can advance my career and be a good wife/significant other.
23. I believe that I can advance my career and be a good mother/friend.
24. I want to advance my career.

If you answered true for beliefs one through nine, or false for ten through twenty-four, then take some time to think back on a memory that correlates with these beliefs.

If you have a hard time thinking of a memory, then try out the "Seven Whys" exercise. First, ask yourself why the belief is true. Then, take your answer and ask why again. Do this a total of seven times to get to the core of your belief. Once you discover where the belief came from, then you can decide to consciously change that belief. Most often, it's helpful to explore God's word and find Bible verses that support your new beliefs.

Start noticing your thoughts, and journal the things that you think about. The more you journal, the more you will get out of the experience. Take time to reflect on your thoughts, and identify if you are thinking about things in the past that you can no longer change, negative thoughts or anxiety about what might happen in the future, moments of joy when you are living in the present moment, ideas, judgments, beliefs, etc.

Harmonizing your heart and renewing your mind takes time, and it isn't something that you can do once and be done with. Continue to journal daily as you look to discover your core beliefs and programs.

PRAYER

Dear Heavenly Father, You formed me in my mother's womb and made me perfectly for Your purposes and for Your will to be done. I thank You for Your never-ending love and for giving me a brilliant mind. Lord, I thank You for the ability to change my mind and for the ability to program the cells of my body for good. Thank You for choosing me and for giving me purpose. Often, I find it hard not to worry, have stress, or experience anxiety. I know that these are not the things that You want for me. I ask for Your grace to allow me to align my mind with my heart. Lord, I ask that You help me to search my mind for the beliefs that are holding me back from living the life that You fully intended me to live. In Jesus' name, Amen.

CHAPTER 5

UNDERSTANDING OUR FREQUENCIES

When God created the world, He made the seen and the unseen. In Hebrews 11:3, we read, "By faith we understand that the universe was formed at God's command, so that what is seen was not made out of what was visible."

Our bodies were once thought to be made up of matter. We now know that we are made up of energy, thanks to major developments in quantum physics in the twentieth century. If you were to look at your hand under a powerful microscope, you would not see flesh or bone. You would see atoms flying around in energy fields. The same is true for everything else in the universe, including the book or device that you are holding right now.

Each person has a unique energy frequency in their bodies and, specifically, their hearts.

EACH PERSON'S HEART FREQUENCY IS MORE DISTINCT THAN OUR FINGERPRINTS.

Like our minds that can be shaped by bad programming, the problem with our frequencies is that they can be interrupted by dissident frequencies that get introduced externally or trapped internally in our bodies.

This causes our frequency to lower. When our frequencies are lowered and interfered with, we create negative energy loops that only work to further suppress our ability to thrive. Low frequencies or trapped energy in the body can drag us down a road of fear, guilt, shame, anxiety, anger, and worry. We live as victims waiting for the next attack and blame external sources for our inability to live the life we want.

In the past, we were told that we are separate entities. We now know that everything is interconnected through energy in a unified field. Our energy directly influences others' energy around us, and the things around us influence our frequency level, positively and negatively. Some things make us stronger, whereas other things lower our frequency and make us weaker.

Things that add to our positive energy are being in nature, eating organic fruits and vegetables, exercising, getting out in the sun, standing barefoot on the ground, using essential oils, prayer, gratitude, encouraging words, positive thoughts, and beautiful pictures. On a human level, we know what it feels like to be lifted up by the presence of others. Being connected in the unseen world is a gift from God. Beyond our senses, there are unlimited potentials. When you increase your energy, you will naturally increase your personal energy field—like a gigantic magnet helping you effortlessly attract the things you want in life.[63]

Most of us have diminished our energy fields, leaving us living in low-frequency states. In these states, we feel the effects of stress hormones that leave us drained and do not allow us to tap into our natural potential.

YOUR PAST IS OVER, NOW

Though I had loving parents, my childhood produced a great deal of stress. It was a secret disaster that I kept buried until right before my thirty-fifth birthday—buried from my parents, family, and friends. For many years I believed the lies that were told to me. I lived in constant fear. I feared the dark, empty houses, clowns, heights, snakes, getting fat, never finding a man, conversations with people (especially talking to boys), lake water, sharks, writing on the board, group work, public speaking, reading aloud, interviewing, tests, driving, and more.

I couldn't bear the thought of people finding out who I was. If they knew my secrets, what would they think of me? I was tarnished trash in my mind. When things didn't go my way, I resolved that it was because of my life's circumstances. I would then blame those circumstances for why I couldn't achieve or do the hard things.

Most of all, I feared failure and that people would find out about my secrets. Fear told me, don't even bother trying, you won't measure up. This was my everyday state of mind, which was deeply rooted in a past I was afraid to confront—a past that stole my joy and kept me small.

This fear was born on what should have been an innocent day hanging out and playing. At the age of six, I was molested for the first time by someone I was close to. Because I was so young, I didn't understand what was happening was wrong. I was told not to tell my parents, but I had no clue that it was wrong. I was so unaware that I taught other people how to "play mommy and daddy," which added to my sense of shame, the kind of shame that can steal your dreams because it consumes your soul.

I wish I could say it only happened once, and I wish I could say that it didn't affect my life, but it affected every second of it until I was nearly thirty-five years old and decided that it no longer had the power to hold me back.

I feel led to share my story now because I want it to be an example for anyone who might feel broken or paralyzed by past trauma. It's not easy to work through these deep wounds and the frequency that comes with them. But you can't change those frequencies if you let the past hold you back. I want you to know that you are enough and that you are capable of anything. It might sound like a cliché. But we are capable of so much more.

WHEN OUR FREQUENCY INCREASES,
SO DOES OUR COURAGE.

Even though we know that the subconscious mind consists of the sum of our past, we must accept that we are not victims, no matter the circumstances. We can be more and do more if we are willing to courageously confront our past to make a better future.

It doesn't matter if you had a perfect upbringing with supportive parents, or you grew up in less than desirable circumstances. You have likely had experiences or made choices that haunt you daily. You may have a past that is so horrible it's hard for anyone else even to imagine. I know many of you reading this book have been a victim of physical, mental, or emotional abuse. Even though I have experienced the same, I still can't begin to imagine the horror so many have endured.

I'm not saying that what you encountered in the past was your fault. In life, many things will happen to us that are not our fault or a cause of our actions, but we are ultimately responsible for our life. For example, say you are in a car wreck and your legs are broken. The wreck was the other person's fault, but that doesn't change the fact that you have to be the one to go through the surgeries and the rehab to learn how to walk again. We don't get to choose our life circumstances, yet we can allow them to be the reason that we remain stuck.

To move into the future, we must release ourselves from the chains of our past.

If you are going to succeed, then you need to remove the victim costume. You may be wearing heavy mental and emotional armor that's keeping your frequency down and ultimately holding you back. Today, I need you to take it off and accept what happens from this point forward is within your control. Your past can no longer own you, and your current situation is not the problem. Your current situation is a fact and an obstacle. Overcoming this obstacle may not be easy, and it's going to be a little scary, but you can overcome it.

If you have accepted Jesus Christ as your Lord and Savior, then your past is forgiven. Accepting Jesus is more than getting a pass to an eternity in Heaven. When we accept Jesus, we are God's sons and daughters and heirs to His inheritance. We have the grace of God right now and have been made righteous through the death, burial, and resurrection of Jesus. When God looks at you, He doesn't see damaged goods; He sees perfection. When we understand and view ourselves how God views us, we can become free from the limits of our past. As it says in Romans 8:1, "Therefore, there is now no condemnation for those who are in Christ Jesus."

ACTIONS TAKEN IN FAITH

- Review your daily thoughts and journal entries to identify the emotional frequencies you are feeling most often. Most people live in the weak frequencies, which causes them to strive in life, even though we have access to the higher emotional frequencies through the fruit of the Holy Spirit.[64] Very few reach the stage of enlightenment like Jesus.

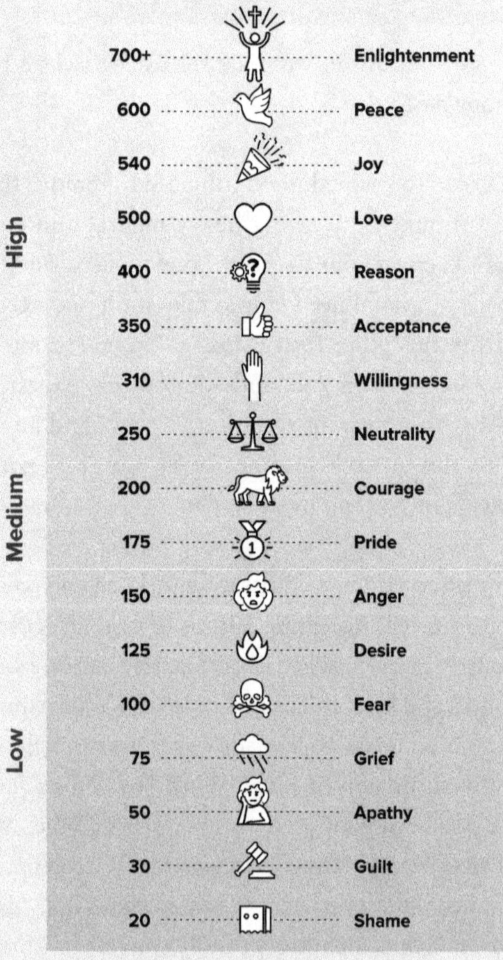

- Increase your frequency
  - Use a grounding mat or take time to walk barefoot outside for at least twenty minutes a day.
  - Drink plenty of clean, filtered water.
  - Get early morning and late afternoon sun.
  - Eat fresh, organic fruits and vegetables.
  - Incorporate your favorite essential oils.
  - Move daily.
  - Take notice of your negative thoughts. When you identify a negative thought, ask yourself, *Is this what God says is true?* If not, then reject the thought and send it away in Jesus' name.
  - Take notice of your automatic feelings—when you are feeling angry, frustrated, overwhelmed, and so on. Remind yourself that you are in control, and try to override the subconscious program. Pray for God's grace to enter in and take over. This is hard to do at first because feelings are strong and come on fast. Plus, we can justify everything that is happening around us if we allow ourselves. Show compassion for yourself, and if you act or react in a way that you wish you wouldn't, take time to reflect on your childhood and life to discover what might be causing this subconscious reaction.

PRAYER

Dear Elohim (The Creator), You are the Most High, and I'm so thankful that You created me in Your image to do Your will. Thank You for allowing me to have access to infinite possibilities through the unseen world. Lord Jesus, I thank You for coming to Earth and sacrificing Yourself so that I may live connected to the Creator and experience the peace that You have always intended for me. Lord, help me to identify and experience the things that will help me to increase my personal frequency so that I may experience peace in my everyday life. Lord, I thank You for allowing me to gain awareness over my thoughts and for the ability not to accept thoughts that are not from You. In Jesus' name I pray, Amen.

CHAPTER 6

UNDERSTANDING OUR GIFTS

When I was first married, I would regularly go out for an evening with my girlfriends. Louis, my husband, would take care of our three children—everything from meals and homework to showers and bedtime routines. When I would arrive home, I would go straight to the kitchen to wash the dishes, clean the counters. I would straighten the pillows in the living room or sort mail. Louis wanted me to relax when I got home, so he started to do the dishes. But for some reason, I couldn't relax: no matter how much Louis did when I got home, I would find what wasn't done and get it organized.

This created tension and even led to arguments. In Louis's mind, I was unable to show gratitude for what he had done. For me, I was grateful and wanted to make up for time away by helping with whatever needed fixing. As time went on, Louis would work to get the entire house spotless, and I knew that it was my job to relax when I got home, as it would leave him feeling underappreciated if I didn't. This went on for years until I became more self-aware, with the understanding that my gifts and talents were not his, that we were wired differently according to God's purpose. When I came home, I learned not to fuss so much, and my husband learned that it wasn't an insult if I started to pick things up.

Ephesians 2:10 says, "For we are his workmanship, created in Christ Jesus for good works, which God prepared beforehand, that we should walk in them" (ESV).

Have you ever doubted your ability because you weren't like someone else? The world teaches us to look around and judge ourselves based on the accomplishments of others. Frequently in life, we are being judged in the context of our peers. We categorize people as smart, dumb, talented, beautiful, jack of all trades, clumsy, athletic, handicap, introverted, extroverted, good speaker, and so forth. It is as if these labels are more predictive of our ultimate success.

Too often these categories lead us to determine what we are capable of before we even try something. This impacts our perception of others too. When we judge ourselves as incapable, we are telling ourselves *no*, thus limiting what God can do through us.

WHEN WE CAN UNDERSTAND HOW AND WHY WE ARE MADE, WE CAN BETTER UNDERSTAND OTHERS.

If you find yourself frustrated or questioning why others are doing what they do, then there is work to do on self-awareness. Self-awareness is defined as conscious knowledge of one's character, feelings, motives, and desires.

Using skill and behavior assessments can help you understand how you are wired and how others are not like you. Behavioral assessments are relatively inexpensive and can help you harness your strengths, become aware of your blind spots, be more perceptive of other unique gifts and strengths, and be more insightful about how others think.

Self-awareness assessments helped me realize how I was wired and freed me from the need to compare myself to other people. According to the DiSC and Enneagram behavioral assessments, I'm a direct perfectionist. Only 3 percent of the population falls under the D or direct category of the DiSC behavioral assessment. The DiSC assessment commonly helps us understand how we communicate and make decisions.[65] The direct personality type is focused on tasks, decisive, direct, results orientated, challenges the status quo, thinks big picture, and likes to be challenged.

Only 8.9 percent of the population are reformers or perfectionists, also known as "one" on the Enneagram, which is an assessment that helps you discover your personality type based on your internal self-talk.[66] Ones like to follow the rules, pay close attention to details, avoid making mistakes, be responsible, have a strong moral compass, and set high standards. Ones strive to be good and honorable. They want to find purpose in their lives, in particular the ability to improve the welfare of people and make things better for the greater good.

It turns out that when my husband said that he never met anyone like me, he was right! I'm not wired like most people. This is why I wanted to tidy up after my husband, and probably would have even if he'd hired a cleaning service to come in while I was out. It doesn't mean he, or the cleaners, would be less than me. It just so happens that one of my strengths leads me to want things more orderly than most.

Gaining self-awareness helped me to become a better mom, friend, daughter, and leader. The results didn't make me look at things that were out of my reach or off limits. Instead, they allowed me to amplify my strengths and to have an awareness of my blind spots. When we know where we are not as gifted, we can work in those areas or build a team to fill those gaps. We can invite the Holy Spirit in to work through us, and with increasing faith, anything will be possible for us. Sometimes God calls us to things that we don't feel naturally gifted in. Paul went around speaking, even though he wasn't considered a good speaker. God used Paul's willingness, and Paul allowed the Holy Spirit to use him to accomplish the will of God. Paul is responsible for writing just over a quarter of the New Testament and leading many people to Christ through his ministry.

1 Peter 4:10 states, "Each of you should use whatever gift you have received to serve others, as faithful stewards of God's grace in its various forms." God designed us all in His image, and He didn't make any of us more valuable than others.

Paul writes in Romans 12:6–8 that "we have different gifts, according to the grace given to each of us. If your gift is prophesying, then prophesy in accordance with your faith; if it is serving, then serve; if it is teaching, then teach; if it is to encourage, then give encouragement; if it is giving, then give generously; if it is to lead, do it diligently; if it is to show mercy, do it cheerfully." God gives us each gifts. It's our job to use those gifts and be good stewards of our gifts. It is our responsibility not to talk badly or diminish the gifts that God has given us. No matter what God has gifted us with, we should work joyfully for the Lord.

The world will tell us that we are less than others based on comparisons, but God created you and me for a purpose. He made you a person of value. He made you uniquely you for His will.

Others may not see your worth, but God does, and if you follow His will for your life, then you, no matter your personality type, will live a great life.

ACTIONS TAKEN IN FAITH

- Take the DiSC and Enneagram assessments mentioned above and, furthermore, go to www.GodsNotDoneWithYouBook.com/bonus
- After reviewing the results, identify and write down your blind spots or the areas you are not currently gifted in.
- Take notice of yourself, and talk about your personality type. Are you embracing who God made you to be? Or are you cursing Him?
- Spend time talking to God about your gifts and how He wants you to use those gifts. If you have been talking negatively about yourself, then ask God to forgive you and thank Him for creating you perfectly for His will.

PRAYER

Dear Heavenly Father, You are the ultimate Creator, and I thank You for creating me in my mother's womb with great love and care. Lord, I thank You for uniquely gifting me for Your will. Lord, I know that I haven't always been kind to myself and that often I have put myself down. Forgive me for not seeing myself and others the way that You view us. Lord, help me to harness my gifts and be a great steward of what You have given me. Lord, I pray that You would continue to bless me with gifts and talents that will assist me in doing Your will, and Lord, in those times when You call me and I feel ill-equipped, I ask that the Holy Spirit would take over and be my strength. Lord, I ask that even in my times of great giftedness and strength that the Holy Spirit would infuse me with even greater strength as I live to do Your will. In Jesus' name, Amen.

CHAPTER 7

UNDERSTANDING OUR BEHAVIORS

This world's demands can leave us stressed out, exhausted, frustrated, angry, and feeling like we can never measure up. For a woman, the demands of personal care, household chores, and childcare can feel overwhelming—even when we have highly supportive and involved spouses. Not to brag, but I imagine my husband is the man that many women dream of having because he does the laundry, taxis the kids, helps with homework, and allows me to get ready in the morning by ensuring the kids are up, dressed, fed, and ready to go on time. He also supports my love of throwing Pinterest parties; he was making balloon arches with yarn way before the fancy plastic balloon arch tape came out.

But as my career was developing, I often found myself defeated by the demands of this world, even with my husband helping. I was irritable, frustrated, and angry a lot of the time. No matter how hard I worked, I couldn't manage to get everything done for our family of six, our home, my career, the community, my friends, and God. This was with a housekeeper, lawn care, and full-time weekly childcare. It didn't matter how much I was doing; I always felt the need to do more. If you told me, "Mary, we will give you four more hours a day," I would have filled those four hours with even more stuff. There was always something more to do: a new training course, a new skill to develop, another project.

One Monday morning, I was getting myself ready for work, and my husband announced that he would take the girls to school. Everyone was joyfully eating and dancing in the kitchen, which we did most mornings when the kids were little. At this point, our oldest daughter needed to catch the city bus, our oldest son was in high school, our youngest daughter was in middle school, and our baby boy was still in daycare—four different directions, with two working parents.

As I looked around, I noticed our baby walking around in his diaper and an unpacked lunchbox. For me to make it to work for the company-wide meeting, I had to be out the door in five minutes. Our son hated riding in the car, and I knew it would take at least ten minutes to wrangle him into his car seat. At that moment, I snapped, sternly telling my baby boy that he had to get dressed *now!* He started crying, and the whole house went up in flames. I melted. What had I done? My poor, innocent baby was put into a situation where he felt afraid, the rest of the kids were frightened, and my husband was angry with me.

I often felt like I was giving my family the scraps of me because I couldn't go full steam at work and keep all the balls in the air without dropping one from time to time.

OUR FAMILIES ARE SUPPOSED TO BE THE ONES THAT WE LOVE THE MOST, AND THEY DESERVE THE BEST OF US, BUT SO OFTEN, THEY BECOME THE ONES THAT GET THE WORN-OUT VERSIONS OF US.

When we live to serve the world and the flesh, there is no rest. There will always be something more that needs to be done, that we should be doing, or that we are supposed to be doing. We start to live urgently, and the most important things go by the wayside. Our health, relationships, and spiritual life suffer, and the cycle gets worse over time.

We start to believe that the only way to make things work is to try harder, leaving us with little time to rest as we go through the motions of trying to do the right things. We find it hard to focus only on the moment. If we are reading our Bibles, we are thinking about work. When we are at work, we are thinking about our kids' needs and dinner. It's a never-ending cycle of exhaustion, frustration, and guilt—leaving us feeling like a failure.

This was me for many years. I would strive to be perfect, hurry to get things done, and achieve more and more. On social media, I had it all put together. At work, I wore a smile, and if you called me on the phone, I was chipper and wonderful. No matter how hard I worked, or how put together I looked, I would come up feeling empty inside.

I couldn't let the world see this side of me. But I also knew that I couldn't continue down this path. Nothing in life was worth my kids feeling afraid of their mom. The problem was I couldn't figure out what was causing this chaos in my life. As I sat pondering where everything had gone off the rails, I was perplexed. In my mind, I had my priorities straight: if you asked me, I would tell you, "God first, husband second, family third, and job fourth."

But if you had looked at my calendar, my family wasn't there—only work: lots and lots of work. There was early morning work, day work, evening work, weekend work, work travel, and working through lunch. At work, I would bring my fullest self as if it were an escape from life. When I got home from work, I would bring my work with me into my family life. Be it conversations or actual work, it was present everywhere. I was trapped in the hamster wheel, and it was spinning fast.

When I would read my Bible, I wasn't connecting with God; I simply checked the God box for the day. When I wrote a nice note to my husband, it was sometimes in vain because I was angry on the inside from something that had happened the previous day. When I read books with my son before bed, I was often more focused on his educational gains with spelling, reading, and writing than on enjoying my time with him. And he wasn't even two.

Over time, I would switch from routine to routine. It became somewhat of a running joke between my husband and me because I would change my behaviors based on the most recent book that I read. No matter how hard or what I tried, behavior modification wasn't working.

Maybe you have been inspired or motivated to try a new routine that could bring some short-term benefit. But eventually you revert to your old ways.

Without consistent success, new inspiration, or continued motivation, the desire to continue the modified behavior diminishes because you are fighting your subconscious programming. Your programming was created to protect you, and no matter how much you say that you want to start that new morning exercise routine, your body tells you that you should remain in your bed sleeping.

Behavior modification rarely works because it works off willpower and is based on continued actions, but what happens when we stop feeling like taking the steps? We fall off the wagon, and we see ourselves as failures. Not knowing that behavior modification doesn't work, we repeatedly try new things, getting the same results. It's like mowing down weeds in the yard and not expecting them to grow again.

REMOVING THE TOP OF THE WEED DOESN'T CHANGE THE ROOT.

This battle continues because we say one thing but deep down in our heart doubt that it's possible for us. It would be nice to lose weight, but internally we doubt that it will actually work. Or we have a belief that there is something wrong with being at a lower weight. Or we have had a traumatic experience that unknowingly still blocks us from getting our desired result.

It's often been said that doing the same thing over and over again, expecting a different result, is the definition of insanity.

To make a lasting difference in our lives, we have to get off the hamster wheel by doing things differently—not only by behavior modification, but by getting to the root of what's causing us to feel frustrated, exhausted, and less than. That is not mowing over the weeds but digging up and removing the weeds' roots so that they don't grow back again.

ACTIONS TAKEN IN FAITH

- In your journal, write down all of the things that you and your kids do. Write down the things that are important to you in life. It could be sports, visits with grandparents, personal care, family vacations, taking coordinated annual family photos, etc.
- Examine the list of items that are written down. Ask yourself, *Why do I do these things*? Do you love them? Are they for your health? Are you supposed to do them, or do you do them out of obligation? Do they bring you joy? Do they make your family's life better? Are they what God wants you to do? Generally, the things that we say we need to do, or were supposed to do, are not things that we should actually do.
- Do a time study for three days and track where you are spending your time. You can write it down or use the calendar on your phone. Track all of your time and be specific during your leisure time. If you are multitasking, then account for both activities. Reflect on where your time is being spent and make changes as needed to make sure you have intentional time for God, your self-care, your husband, and your kids—or if you're not married or don't have children, your friends.

PRAYER

Dear Abba, You are a good and faithful Father. Thank You for freeing me from needing to live up to worldly standards. Lord, I ask that You help me to be intentional with the time that You have given me and allow me to be fully present in the moment. Lord, I ask that You take away the stress that the world places on me and my family to live up to its ideals. I thank You for making me more aware of my roles and for freeing me from needing to fix and control others and the world around me. I know that I haven't always placed You first, Lord, and sometimes I've seen it as a chore to spend time with You. Lord, I ask that You forgive me for the times that I have plugged too many things into my schedule that caused me to squeeze my time with You and my family. I love You, God, and recommit myself to living for You. In Jesus' name, Amen.

CHAPTER 8

THE POWER OF OUR THOUGHTS AND WORDS

When God created the universe, He created it first in thoughts and then with words. As Psalm 33:6 says, "By the word of the Lord the heavens were made, and by the breath of his mouth all their host" (New Living Translation). The famous account in Genesis tells us of a "formless and empty" earth "where darkness covered the deep waters" until "God said, 'Let there be light,' and there was light." The phrase "then God said" is echoed eight more times in Genesis, as God creates the universe in six days—through intention with words.[67]

You've heard the old phrase "sticks and stones may break my bones, but words will never hurt me." It's easy for us to say this as a kid and puff our chest out like words don't bother us. But we know that's not true.

> WORDS HAVE THE POWER TO BRING LIFE OR DEATH.[68]

Like our mind and body, words possess energy too. All of our thoughts and words impact us and the world. When we think or speak, we emit energy into the field, affecting everything around us.

Experiments have been done on plants in which each plant was given equal parts water and sunlight, but they were each intentionally spoken to and thought about differently. One plant is designated the ugly plant, and participants in this experiment are to think and say negative things to it. The other plant is the pretty plant, and the participants say and think loving and caring thoughts about it.[69] After a few weeks, the plant being told and thought about negatively will look as if it's dying. On the other hand, the loved plant will look beautiful and healthy.

It seems strange this would work, but other experiments conducted on objects like cooked rice have shown similar results.[70] Rice that's been praised in a container holds up much better than rice that's been ridiculed. The ridiculed rice is more likely to mold. Negative words with negative emotions literally rot and destroy.

This message is clear throughout the Bible.

In Proverbs 15:4, we hear how "gentle words bring life and health; a deceitful tongue crushes the spirit," in 16:24, "Kind words are like honey—sweet to the soul and healthy for the body," and in 18:4, "A person's words can be life-giving water; words of true wisdom are as refreshing as a bubbling brook" (NLT).

Similar studies have been done on water—using thoughts, prayer photos, and music. The water shown, told, prayed over, or thought about with positive words will form beautiful ice crystals when frozen, but the water told, shown, thought about, prayed over, or told negative things freezes into a jagged crystal.[71] You should go and look this up right now so you can see for yourself. Our words and thoughts matter. If we fill our life with negative words or thoughts, they will shape our identity. The opposite is also true.

Henry Ford famously said, "Whether you think that you can, or you think that you can't, you are right."

Most people are trapped in negative thought loops. Over time our brains are trained to think negative thoughts and recall negative memories naturally. Fear runs rampant throughout our minds—fear of failure, rejection, missing out, being hurt, and so on. We think about the stressful things, our appearance and weight, mistakes we've made, people who hurt us, the people we hurt, worry about what others think, and place judgment on others' actions that negatively impact our thoughts.

It sometimes feels like you can't escape. Maybe you have tried to turn it off and think positively, but you can't. No matter how hard you try, the negative words and thoughts keep rushing back in. You feel cornered, no matter where you go, making it hard to ever be in the present and enjoying the moment. Instead, your mind wanders to the past with worry and the future with anxiety because of the uncertainty. Negative thoughts and words keep us from living at our highest potential, always waiting for the other shoe to drop or not putting ourselves out there because the risk outweighs the reward.

If we can think better thoughts and speak more positively, then we can create better energy. When our energy is positive, people will more naturally want to be around us, and our confidence will increase. You are the only one who can control your thoughts. Think about it for a second. No one else can think or speak for you. Sure, people can influence your thoughts, but they cannot actually make you think a thought.

The way you perceive and speak about someone's actions is within your control. If you fill your mind with thoughts or stories that cause anger, worry, fear, and anxiety, that's the energy you'll produce. Say someone cuts you off in traffic. You could think they are a jerk and need to learn how to drive. Or you could think they must have somewhere important to go: *I hope they make it in time.*

God tells us, in Matthew, that the measurement in which we judge others will be the way we will be judged. When we are caught up in judgment, we determine why or what others' motives and intentions are, creating stories in our minds and then using this information in the future as fact.[72] Judgment, resentment, and unforgiveness all cause us to think negatively. When we think negatively, we are lowering our energy. When we choose not to forgive, we think that we are punishing the other person, and to a small degree, we are, since we are thinking negatively about them, but more than that, we are flooding our own body with stress chemicals. It's like drinking a vial of poison and expecting the other person to suffer.

Viktor Frankl, a neurologist and Holocaust survivor, said this after observing the prisoners' differences in the concentration camps. "Everything can be taken from a man but one thing: the last of the human freedoms—to choose one's attitude in any given set of circumstances, to choose one's own way."[73]

No matter what your circumstances, you can choose a different way. One of the best ways to rewire your thinking and speaking is to practice gratitude.

We introduced this in our family life through a gratitude report we added during bedtime to our youngest son, Dalton. A "gratitude report" consists of us taking turns saying three things that we are grateful for. It's a great way to end the day, gain insight into your child's world, all while increasing your happiness too. Practicing gratitude has been linked to higher levels of happiness.[74] Happy people have more energy. People with more energy accomplish more and are viewed as more confident and likable.

You can begin now by listing in your journal three things you're grateful for. Do this every day.

On occasion, people will have a hard time thinking of things that they are grateful for. The key is not to find jackpots of gratitude but to simply find gratitude in everyday life. Things like water, health, shelter, family, friends, and pets are great things to be grateful for.

PAUL TELLS US, IN 1 THESSALONIANS 5:18, "GIVE THANKS IN ALL CIRCUMSTANCES; FOR THIS IS THE WILL OF GOD IN CHRIST JESUS FOR YOU."

Sometimes we get confused because we substitute the word "in" and replace it with "for." God is not telling us that we have to be thankful "for all circumstances." There are many times in life that we are in terrible situations, but no matter what is occurring, we can give thanks to God amid the situation.

In the New Testament, giving thanks is mentioned seventy-two times. This thanksgiving isn't a simple thank you for doing something, but rather an outpouring of praise for who God is and what He has done. According to Dr. Daniel Amen, a world-renowned neurologist, after practicing gratitude daily, you will start to change your brain's patterns and become a happier person.[75] When we show gratitude or thanksgiving, our mind registers these events as already happening.

Most often, we give thanks after the fact. We thank God after we have received something or after something good happens. When we practice gratitude in this limited way, we miss out on the greatest blessings. We limit our blessings to what we have already received. To tap into our future, we can be thankful for things that haven't yet occurred. When you show gratitude for future events, you draw them into the realm of possibility for yourself.

God created the world first with a thought and then through words. Thoughts and words are two of the most powerful resources that we have in living a life of abundance. It's up to us to interpret the world around us. We have a choice to speak abundance into our lives. To fully embrace the power of our words and thoughts, we need to reframe our world and take control of our perspective of the world. Your body is an incredible gift that benefits instantly from positive words and thoughts.

ACTIONS TAKEN IN FAITH

- Each day write down at least three things that you are thankful for and make at least one of them something that hasn't yet occurred. This simple exercise will increase your happiness and draw you closer to your future.
- Search your heart for unforgiveness, resentment, and bitterness. In your journal, write down the issues and people that you need to release from your past. Take time to pray and forgive yourself and others. If you need to ask others for forgiveness, then do that this week. As scary as it is, you will be glad that you did.
- Think about relationships that you want to improve in your life. Reflect on the way that you think and talk about the other person. Start to talk and think positively about them. This will not change the other person initially, but it will change the lens in which you see the other person. Don't wait for the other person to change or deserve you to think or speak positively about them.
- Take time to think about the words and thoughts that you have around advancing your career. Take time to write in your journal all of the positive things that will happen for you, your family, and your company because you have advanced.

PRAYER

Dear Heavenly Father, I thank You for being my Creator and for giving me so many things to be grateful for. I thank You for my current career. Lord, I pray that You will help me to remain humble in my current position so that I am able to be promoted when it is Your will and in accordance with Your purpose. I thank You for giving me tools to renew my mind and for sending Jesus to die so that I can have a direct and constant relationship with You. I thank You for Your love and forgiveness, Lord. I ask that You help me to forgive others that have wronged me and that You help me to have self-forgiveness for those that I have hurt. Lord, I pray for those that are against me that their hearts may be softened and that they turn their wrath away. I invite You deep into my heart to search it thoroughly to find any bitterness, envy, or resentment that I might be harboring that is causing me to live a life that is less than what You created for me. Lord, help me to show love to others by thinking and speaking positively about others. Lord, please forgive me for the times that I have gossiped or was critical of others. Lord, I ask that You help me find joy and praise You in all circumstances, for where You are, there is plenty to praise. In Jesus' name, Amen.

CHAPTER 9

FEELINGS, EMOTIONS, AND THE HEART

Feelings and emotions are commonly thought to be synonymous, but our emotions and feelings are created and felt differently. Feelings come about subconsciously and then are felt all over our bodies. This is happening at the cellular level. Our cells have memories. Feelings are felt through frequencies that are stored in our subconscious minds. They replay the past for us over and over again. If you were to think about a past painful memory, your body chemistry would change, and you will go back and experience the same chemical experience associated with your memory. By replaying our memories, we make them more real. If we have an experience similar to the stored experience, our bodies will produce the same feelings.

This is the same for positive memories. Think about a time spent looking at old photos from a joyful time in your life. Looking at the pictures activated the old memories, and you smiled and were filled with joy.

When we store negative emotional frequencies in our bodies,

we can feel something is off. But over time we start to ignore the feelings even though they never went away. It's the emotion that has the power to override or create new stored feelings. When someone says something mean to us, we can choose not to absorb the negative by sending the thought away, and thus, controlling the emotion instead of letting it control us. This takes time to master. But once you can clearly process what was said without taking it personally, then you no longer store that emotional frequency. This is why God tells us to forgive.

FORGIVENESS IS NOT ONLY FOR THE OTHER PERSON.

It's for you too. When you harbor negative emotions, you are lowering your frequencies. Low frequencies, also known as dissident frequencies, over time will cause the cells in your body to become weak and diseased.

When you have weak cells in your body, you are more prone to injury, and illness too. People who live with low frequency and stress are also known not only to age faster but to live shorter lives.

If the mind is where we develop our programmed responses to the world around us, the heart is where we store our personal identity. What is in our hearts is what we produce in our lives. Proverbs 27:19 says, "As water reflects the face, so one's life reflects the heart."

This is why God tells us time and time again to guard our hearts. Proverbs 4:23 also says, "Above all else, guard your heart, for everything you do flows from it." A good man brings good things out of the good stored up in his heart, and an evil man brings evil things out of the evil stored up in his heart. For the mouth speaks what the heart is full of.[76]

When we adopt beliefs about ourselves, they live in our hearts, and what is in our hearts, we create in our lives. You reap what you sow. If you store up anger, bitterness, resentment, lack, and frustration, you will create those things in your life.

The Law of Reaping and Sowing

When we store up "love, joy, peace, patience, kindness, goodness, faithfulness, gentleness, and self-control," we will produce these things in our lives. God calls these harvests the fruit of the Spirit in Galatians 5:22 (ESV). Whether you are a follower of Jesus Christ or not, the principle works the same way. Garbage in, garbage out. Good in, good out. You cannot sow a kernel of corn and produce a fruit tree. The same way you cannot have fear in your heart and live in peace.

> AS CHRISTIANS, EACH OF US HAS THE HOLY SPIRIT LIVING INSIDE OF OUR HEARTS, TRYING TO TALK TO US.

Most of us cannot hear the Holy Spirit because we don't take the time to listen, don't clearly understand His role, don't fully accept what Jesus did for us on the cross, or drown out the voice with our self-doubt. If you have been saved, you may have noticed you were a different person for a while. The Holy Spirit filled your heart. For many, that's all that happens. Our hearts are filled, but our minds are never renewed.

Jesus illustrates this point in the parable of the sower and the seed, from the Gospel of Matthew, chapter 13. The seed is the word or message of God, and the ground or the soil is your heart. When you accept Jesus into your heart, if you don't develop a stronger root and a renewed mind, then you are still saved because you believe, but you will never fully experience the abundant promises and peace that God gave you as an heir of Christ. The parable is about seed falling on the path, in rocky places, and amongst thorns. These areas represent life circumstances that we allow to take precedent over the promises of God.

> Listen then to what the parable of the sower means: When anyone hears the message about the kingdom and does not understand it, the evil one comes and snatches away what was sown in their heart. This is the seed sown along the path. The seed falling on rocky ground refers to someone who hears the word and at once receives it with joy. But since they have no root, they last only a short time. When trouble or persecution comes because of the word, they quickly fall away. The seed falling among the thorns refers to someone who hears the word, but the worries of this life and the deceitfulness of wealth choke the word, making it unfruitful. But the seed falling on good soil refers to someone who hears the word and understands it. This is the one who produces a crop, yielding a hundred, sixty or thirty times what was sown.[77]

This parable shows us that we enter the Kingdom of God through our heart. So it's important that we examine our core beliefs, motives, priorities, and intentions.

Entering the Kingdom of God

We enter the Kingdom of God

After being saved, I decided not to work at a brewery where so many people were under the influence of alcohol. It was a wonderful company, with beautiful people and incredible opportunities, but it no longer aligned with my values. It no longer felt like the place where I should be sowing my own seeds.

When we focus our hearts on the things God calls us to, we can find rest and peace in all areas of our lives.

God provides us with the great commandment in John 13:34: "Love one another. As I have loved you, so you must love one another."

In Matthew 6:33, Jesus says, "But seek first his kingdom and his righteousness, and all these things will be given to you as well."

When we seek a relationship with God and do His will, we will have more peace, joy, love, self-control, gentleness, kindness, patience, and faithfulness in our lives.

Lens Through the World

Lens Through Christ

We cannot give what we do not have stored up in our hearts. This is why we need to daily surrender to God in prayer and thanksgiving, study scriptures, and experience the fullness of God's covenant with Jesus in our lives.

ACTIONS TAKEN IN FAITH

- Take notice when others speak to you. Ask yourself if what they are saying is true in God's eyes. If it's not, then send away the thought and do not let the emotion take root in your heart.
- Stop judging others and get curious. We can't know why people do things unless we ask them. Ask questions to gain understanding and trust that they are being honest when they tell you their motives. Start assuming that others are not acting to hurt you, but rather for your good or out of their own fears.
- Take control of your thoughts. If you notice yourself thinking negative thoughts, then remind yourself that they are not from God, and say what is true.
- Pray daily upon waking for the Holy Spirit to work through you to do God's will.

PRAYER

Dear Heavenly Father, You are the Most High, and Your words and thoughts are only good and pure. Lord Jesus, there have been many times when I've looked at people in the world, and all I've seen were their blemishes. I've gossiped and have often looked for others' flaws as a way to make myself feel better. There have been times when I've assumed the actions of others, and I'm sorry, Lord. Jesus, I ask that You help me to reframe the way that I see others. Let me always see the best in others and always assume the best in others. Lord, help me to be more like Jesus so that I can live in peace without absorbing the painful critics of this world. Lord, I ask that You soften the hearts of those that want to see me suffer so that they would one day have a relationship with You too, Lord. Lord, I thank You for my freedom to choose my thoughts and my reactions to the world around me. Lord, each day as I wake, I surrender to You and ask that You would allow me to be in the present moment and think only of things that strengthen my body and soul. May all of this be done in Jesus' name so that I can live each day to the fullest as I do Your will. Amen.

CHAPTER 10

BELIEFS

When I was six years old and in the first grade, I struggled terribly with spelling, reading, and writing. I have no memory of passing a single spelling test. Each week the teacher would give us a new list of words, and I would study nightly with my mother at the kitchen table. My mom should get awards for the time she spent trying to help, but it was to no avail. I couldn't learn to spell—even simple words. My mother would eventually get frustrated. I don't blame her; it was a maddening situation.

The test day would inevitably come, and I would fail over and over again. I can still remember the half sheets of paper numbered down the side with red splashes everywhere and large Ds and Fs in the top corner. I hated myself for being so stupid and was extremely embarrassed when I got my test back. The other kids would talk to one another, celebrating their scores, and I sat in my chair quietly, with my head down, trying to act invisible.

That year I lost out on movie and popcorn days because I couldn't spell. I felt like a total failure. From that point forward, I created a negative belief that shaped my life. My insecurity plagued me all through school. I had special tutors, assistants, and small groups that pulled me out of normal class routines. There were different worksheets, games, and techniques for me, but nothing worked.

Over the years, I didn't get any better and continued to tell myself and others how terrible I was. For most of my life, it has set limits on what I could do. I wanted to be better, but deep down, I didn't believe I could be. My defense as an adult was to avoid situations where I would be embarrassed.

OVER TIME, OUR THOUGHTS AND WORDS FURTHER REINFORCE OUR BELIEFS, MAKING THEM STRONGER AND STRONGER.

The things you believe about yourself become your identity. What we believe and, more importantly, what we believe about ourselves set the limits for what we can achieve in life.

If you take a moment to think about your past, you can likely think of a time when you didn't believe in yourself, and then all of a sudden, you became inspired and changed that belief and were able to accomplish something you once thought to be impossible.

Our limiting beliefs can be a product of the subconscious mind passed down to us, a new belief we adopted because of an experience, or the result of someone else's lack of belief in us.

If you are like me, you likely have more than one limiting belief in your life that keeps you from living at your highest potential. Many women do not believe they are capable of being a CEO or an executive. This leads us to sabotage ourselves by saying we are not interested in an executive position. We won't bother trying because we don't believe it's possible. It's not that becoming an executive should be how we measure a successful career. But I wonder how many women are counting themselves out before they even try.

I know I was one of them. Remember, I didn't believe I could be a COO. But when I changed my beliefs and said at a leadership meeting that I would be the next COO, it happened four months later. If I hadn't changed my belief, I wouldn't have walked into my manager's office to ask for the position.

A lack of belief in ourselves is the number-one thing holding us back. We have been taught to be realistic, be responsible, and use common sense, but this is not how the power of belief works. Many of our beliefs that hold us back cause us to play the victim in our own lives. We don't believe we have access to the same opportunities as other people because of something that occurred in our lives. It's easy to get caught up in victim mode without even realizing it. We program our personal beliefs in our heart when we use the words I am, I'm not, and I can't.

Belief, which is an expression of faith, is when your thoughts and feelings harmonize. Where there is belief or faith, there cannot be doubt or wavering.[78] Any belief that causes you to stumble, strive, or stress is not from God.

Faith Equation

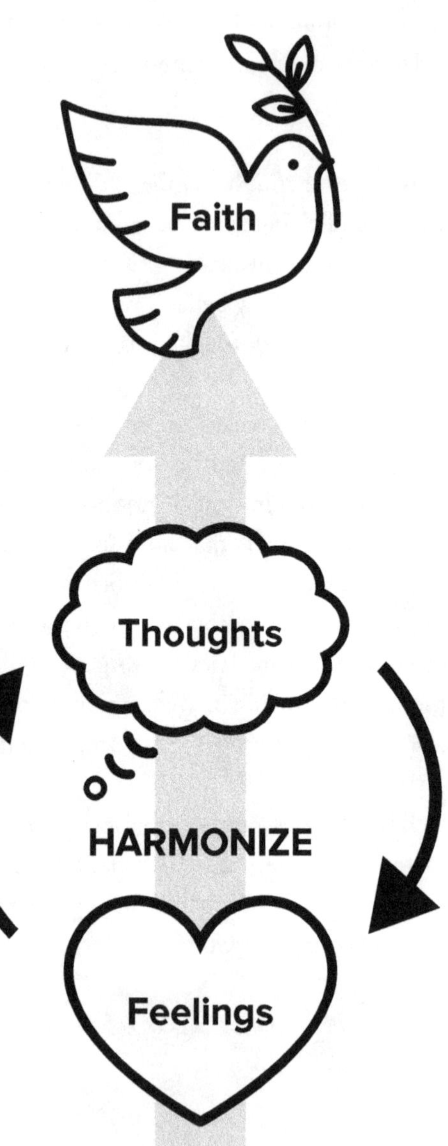

Have you ever made one of these statements as to why you are not capable? *But I'm too old, not old enough, not smart enough, too smart for that, introverted, extroverted, not organized, not strong enough, too strong, a mom, a girl, too fat, too skinny.* Or *I don't have enough money, time, skills, help*. Or *I don't know how to market, make sales, talk to people, lead a team, work on a computer, read, write, spell, or run.* Or *I don't like swimming, running, reading.* Or *I don't want to manage others, have a million dollars, live in a big home, wear dress clothes to work*, etc. Add in any statement that limits you because of your physical appearance, mental aptitude, physical ability, current financial position, or basic life needs.

These statements that we make about ourselves are honest. But few people realize the impact that such statements have on the heart. When we make these statements, we own them as our identity.

Sometimes our self-identifying statements that shape our beliefs come from external influences. News, TV, advertisements, and social media contribute to our beliefs and standards. As women, we feel this in what we hear about being in the workplace, staying at home, or who should be the primary breadwinner in a marriage. Maybe you are a minority and have been told that you are disadvantaged because of it.

WHAT WE BELIEVE IS SHAPED BY EVERY EXPERIENCE AND INPUT WE'VE HAD IN LIFE.

Growing up, my older sister was always better than me at everything except three things—babysitting, art, and volleyball. She was my role model and example of what I was capable of achieving. God blessed me with height, and basketball was the family sport. In my mind, my sister was always the better basketball player, and I wasn't capable of being better than she was. When she decided not to continue playing basketball in college, I didn't believe that I was capable either. So I never even tried.

In 1945, Gunder Hagg set the best time for running a mile at 4:01.4. After he set this record, it was said to be impossible to run a sub-four-minute mile. That was until nine years later, when Roger Bannister broke the record and changed the world's belief. After Bannister broke the record, it took only seven weeks for his record to be broken.[79] Today, over 1,500 athletes from around the world have broken the four-minute barrier.[80] Runners didn't all of a sudden learn a new way of running. They had a new belief.

Your beliefs create your life or reality. If you want something different in life, you must first believe that it is possible.

THE POWER OF "I AM"

In Exodus 3:14, God said to Moses, "I Am Who I Am." And He said, "Say this to the people of Israel, 'I Am has sent me to you'" (NLT). The power of these two words is infinite. First, they can help us to identify who God is.

God says, "I am who I am." Today, we create our identities by saying things like I am a woman, I am a mother, I am a good friend, I am a (insert your position at work), etc. When God gives a name for His people to call Him, it conveys His dominion over all things, the source of His power, and His eternal nature: I AM. He is the self-sufficient, self-sustaining God who was, who is, and who will be.

In John 8:58, Jesus said to His disciples, "I tell you the truth, before Abraham was even born, I Am!" (NLT)

Seven more times in the book of John, Jesus uses the phrase "I Am" in the Bible. Each time, He uses the words He is referring to a positive and life-giving truth. He tells the world who He is. I Am, The Light of the World, The Door, The Bread of Life, Good Shepherd, The Resurrection and Life, The Vine, The Way, and the Truth and the Life.[81]

These powerful statements teach us about the character of God. The words "I am" are powerful in our lives too. We discussed earlier about using self-identifying statements and how they had the power to change your life for better or worse.

In order to start changing your beliefs about yourself, we will use affirmations. An affirmation is a positive life-giving statement that you say about something that you want to become true. Affirmations help you overcome challenges and avoid self-sabotaging behaviors. Often, we get trapped in our negative thoughts that sabotage us.

When repeated frequently, your mind will start to believe in them and you will notice positive changes. At first, your affirmations may feel like wishes. But with time, they will become reality.

Since our thoughts create our reality, it doesn't matter if the affirmation is true yet or not. We are simply programming our minds with the thoughts that we want to believe will draw us closer to our desired life. Imagine your mind is like a bank account. Positive thoughts are deposits, and negative thoughts are withdrawals. Right now, your bank account may be overdrawn, but each day that you input positive affirmations, you make deposits into the account.

YOU CANNOT WAIT FOR YOUR BANK ACCOUNT TO BE FULL TO MAKE A DEPOSIT.

In the same way, you can't wait for something to happen in order to decide that you want it. You have to desire and believe it first before you get it.

Each day we get to choose our thoughts and the way that we respond to circumstances. When your subconscious mind is reprogrammed with positive thoughts, you will have more confidence.

If you take a moment to recall some of your past successes, you will notice that those successes most often came because of the faith or confidence you had. Through affirmations you strengthen your neural pathways, allowing you to respond to challenges with courage. Take a few minutes and write down a list of past accomplishments. You can refer to this list if you are feeling discouraged. Many times, we don't remember or discount how many things we have accomplished.

EXAMPLES OF "I AM" AFFIRMATIONS

- I am more valuable at work than ever before. Each day, I add tremendous value, and I am ready to advance my career. I feel confident, grateful, and humbled for the opportunities that come my way.
- I am an heir of Jesus, and I fully accept the gifts that God has freely given me. I am easily able to surrender to God and experience the fullness of God's grace.

- I am free of the fear of failure. Failure is a good and necessary means to success. I know that God uses every trial I have to produce something even greater. Failure doesn't define me or set limits for what I am capable of doing. This makes me feel grateful for God's love and safe in His arms.
- I am confident, hardworking, and ready to be promoted to the XYZ position. I feel deep gratitude for the opportunity.
- I am intelligent and deserving of more in life. This makes me feel confident and smart. Abundance and wealth are both positive and necessary parts of life.
- I am prosperous, and I find it easy to become more and more prosperous. I do good things with my prosperity; helping both myself and others with money makes me feel confident and joyful.
- I am healthy and do things that are good for my body. I feel energized and capable of taking on any task that comes before me. I feel peaceful.
- I am open to opportunities, and they are abundant in my life. With confidence, I take action on the opportunities that are in front of me. I feel courageous and grateful.
- I am a world-class leader, and my skills continue to improve. My leadership skills inspire others, and that makes me feel proud and kind.
- I am capable of having a thriving career, being a loving wife, and being a great mom (or, if you're single, being a great friend). Being successful in one area does not make me less successful in another. I feel blessed and grateful to have been given so much.

There is no magical number of affirmations. But five or fewer is good so you can repeat them daily. Over time, your beliefs will change, and you will no longer need the affirmation. Once you get connected to your heart, you will just know that you no longer need the affirmation and can add in different ones.

When you write your affirmations, state what you already have with confidence. Starting the affirmations with "I am" does this in a powerful way.

An affirmation should never be written as *I want to become* or *I will*…When we use this language, we tell our bodies and hearts that we do not already have these things.

Add the emotion or feeling that you want to experience, which will send that positive frequency to your body.

ACTIONS TAKEN IN FAITH

- Take time to reflect on your past experiences and beliefs. In your journal, write down beliefs that you have accepted over the years that you want to change. By identifying your beliefs, you can start to rewrite them.
- Once you've written down your five affirmations, take time to read them aloud slowly while recording them. You can use your phone or a handheld recorder. After reading each affirmation, picture yourself acting out the affirmation. Listen to your recording two times per day—in the morning when you wake up and right before bed at night. It's best if you're in a relaxed state. Change your affirmations over time as needed. Try to keep your recording brief, a couple of minutes long. The key is to repeat the affirmations frequently with firm belief.

PRAYER

Dear Heavenly Father, You are the original and Most High I Am. Lord, I ask that You search my heart, body, and mind for any beliefs that I have accepted that are not from You. You are the only one that can define me and give me my value. Lord, help me to love and see myself the way that You love and see me. Lord, I ask that You would bring a deep peace into my life as I continue to release the past that once held me back from living life the way that You created it for me. In Jesus' name, Amen.

CHAPTER 11

CHANGING YOUR BELIEFS

I'm not a runner—definitely not the 1,500th person to break the four-minute mile. I hate running. I said those words a thousand times before I found myself volunteering with KLOVE at a Fit SA event. When I got there, I was perplexed. The runners looked like ordinary everyday people, not the super athletes I had always envisioned running races. After setting up the booth, our director told us that we would have thirty minutes to wait before the runners got back.

At that moment, I believed that I could, in fact, run. So I took off and ran my first 5K. Three weeks later, I signed up for my first full marathon with four months to train for it. All that it takes to accomplish something is a new belief, a decision, faith, and perseverance.

Over the years of coaching countless entrepreneurial functional medicine practitioners, it was clear that the practitioners who succeeded were those who believed they would. It's not about who is smartest, most talented, went to the best school, has the most money, the type of degree, or is the prettiest.

THE MOST COMMON DENOMINATOR IS A CLEAR DECISION TO BE SUCCESSFUL.

Beliefs can be a spur-of-the-moment decision, built out of devastation or consciously committed to.

The power of the Holy Spirit is part of the inheritance of Jesus through the new covenant. To access this power, you must believe in the death, burial, and resurrection of Jesus. This is a choice that we freely make. God doesn't make you accept Jesus into your heart. He simply knocks and waits at the door.[82] He has done all of the heavy lifting. All that is required of us is to take the last step and open the door. God cannot open the door for you; it's a choice.

Everything that we do in life is a choice. Your life is the sum total of your choices. We all have choices in our careers, relationships, finances, health, generosity, thoughts, words, and attitudes. Our free will allows us to choose anything that we want. Rather than acknowledging this fact, we place limits on our lives by blaming outside influences. We allow our current circumstances and our past to oppress us from living our most abundant lives. We focus on lack, pain, and injustice as reasons we can't live a life greater than our current reality. We settle for what the world says we can have in this life, never realizing the abundance of what God has waiting for us to access now. God never holds things back from us. We are not waiting for God to give us what He said that He would provide us with. He has already given it to us. We are not experiencing it in our lives because we have not believed in it. Belief is a choice that God can't make for us.

We must come to God and believe that we have received His promises now. When we believe that we have the promises of God in our hearts, then we will operate out of faith and love according to God's word. If we believe that we have authority, our faith is in who He says that we are, what He says that we can do, and what He says is ours. For example, He has already forgiven you, but if you don't forgive yourself, you will be unable to experience the peace that forgiveness brings.

Some people believe that because God is in control, they must wait on Him. I believe that God is often waiting on *us*. He's ready to use you and is waiting for *you* to be ready.

We must see ourselves the way God sees us. Many people think that God is angry, wicked, and condemning. But He is none of these things. Through the peace covenant of Jesus, we have been made righteous. No matter what we have done, God right now sees us without blemish and made perfectly for His purpose. We must view ourselves in the same way; otherwise, we are doubting the finished work of Jesus and will never experience the full benefit of the sacrifice God has made.

God operates under a set of truths. Once God has spoken a truth, He cannot go back on His word. If He did, He would be a liar, and no one would trust Him. When He put us on the earth, He gave us authority; this is the same authority that Jesus used when He walked the earth. Many people believe that Jesus was acting with the authority of God and was free from temptation. When Jesus came to Earth, He was fully man, and He was fully God. That's 100 percent each, but the authority that He used on Earth was not that of God.[83]

We see Jesus continually going away in prayer and yielding to the Holy Spirit. Jesus' power came from the Holy Spirit. You have access to this same power in your life, but as Jesus did, you must yield to the Holy Spirit and ask in prayer faithfully to have access to the Holy Spirit.

When we accept what Jesus did through the death, burial, and resurrection, we can activate grace through surrender. When we surrender to God in prayer and ask Him for help, He will aid us. We first must set our pride aside. We must be willing to admit that we need/want help. Going to God for help isn't something that we need to do because we lack intellectual intelligence, although sometimes this will be the case. God tells us to be humble. Part of this humbleness is surrendering to God and asking for His grace even in the things that we feel highly skilled in—not because we are not enough, but because we understand and accept the powerful gift of God's grace. God is like the supercharger cord for your phone and can help you faster and with more ease.

It's a choice to surrender. God is always willing, but we are not always willing. When we surrender, we activate powerful energy that can supply us more than we ever imagined. Remember, we live in an interactive universe where science tells us it's being shaped by our beliefs, perceptions, and intentions. Because God created us with authority, He has given us the freedom to make choices. Some of our choices bring us closer to the things that we want in our lives. Other choices drive us further from our desired life. We often fail to recognize that God made us in His image, and He sent His Son to save us, model His character, and show us how we could function if we accepted Jesus as the standard.

It is a choice to believe that you can have a life of peace, love, and joy that God created for you. We cannot expect to have this life if we don't know what it is we desire: a renewed mind rooted in the promises of God and a heart yielded to the Holy Spirit.

For any belief to work, we have to change our mentality, so we're no longer being influenced by our doubts. The first step is to have a clear desire that is accompanied by a clear why or purpose. God gives you the desires of your heart. Psalm 37:4 says to "take delight in the LORD, and he will give you the desires of your heart." What is it that you are telling God that you desire for your career?

Step two is to make a decision to have faith no matter what. Matthew 21:22 reminds us that "you can pray for anything, and if you have faith, you will receive it" (NLT). You cannot have a plan B or an I'll-try-this-until attitude. Having faith means harmonizing your thoughts, words, heart beliefs, and actions. It's not that you have to be perfect or never have doubt. But the more you align with faith, the easier it is for you to receive.

The third step is to make a plan. Proverbs 21:5 tells us, "The plans of the diligent lead to profit as surely as haste leads to poverty." Realize that you will be shifting priorities to achieve your new belief. To get my runs in, I had to wake up earlier and shift my weekend schedule.

The fourth step is to consistently act upon your plan with faith and hope. James 2:26 says, "Just as the body is dead without breath, so also faith is dead without good works" (NLT).

Steps to Creating Beliefs

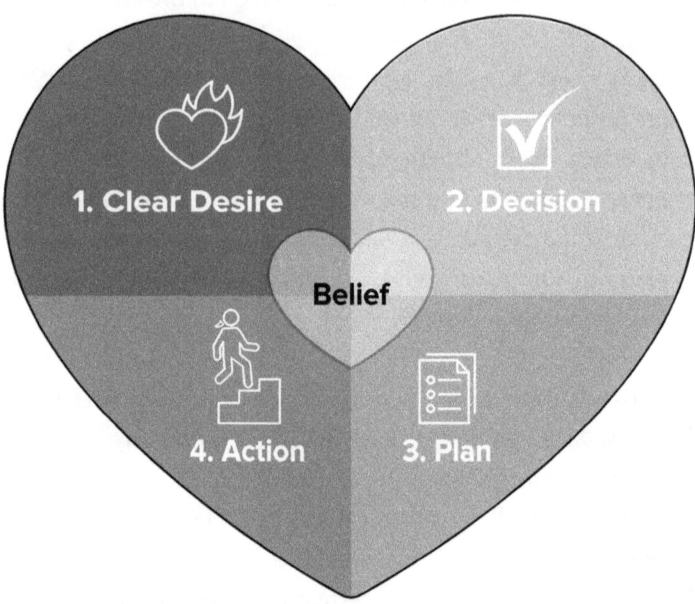

As you take action on your belief, you will build evidence toward the belief; it will become your reality.

To get the evidence, you must decide first. You cannot wait to be ready. Take, for example, running a marathon. I had only ever run three miles when I made this decision. Had I not decided to run a marathon, I don't believe that I would have endured twenty-mile practice runs in the rain, being chased by deer, lying on the side of the road with leg cramps, and nearly being hit by cars in the dark of the early morning. My bed would have taken precedence over trying to run. The decision to run a marathon came at the same time I found out my IVF baby dreams had been put on pause. For me running was a way to get my body in better shape before conceiving and a way to shift my focus from the daily thoughts of infertility.

The same is true for your career. You cannot obtain a career that you do not believe that you can have.

Korn Ferry conducted a research study and interviewed fifty-seven women CEOs. They lead Fortune 1000 companies and large privately held firms. Of the fifty-seven women interviewed, only five of them knew that they wanted to be a CEO; three of them never wanted to be the CEO but felt a need to fulfill the call. Two-thirds of the CEOs said they didn't know that they could be until someone else told them they could be.[84] If you have never been told that you can be an executive, I'm here to tell you that I believe that you can be.

When I tell people that all they need to do is start believing, they are most often skeptical that it will work. You might be skeptical, and that's an entirely normal reaction to new information. I would encourage you to continue studying this topic.

THE PLACEBO EFFECT IS A STRONG INDICATION THAT WHAT WE BELIEVE HAS A HUGE IMPACT ON OUR REALITY.

Nearly 35 percent of all results are attributed to the placebo effect.[85] In a blind study with cancer patients undergoing chemotherapy, 30 percent of the placebo group, the group that wasn't given radiation, lost their hair.[86] Only the belief that they would lose their hair was enough to cause them to.

There are countless other placebo studies done where people recovered completely from fake knee surgeries (patients were put under anesthesia, a cut was made, and then they were stitched back up) to saline given as morphine to reduce pain. Dr. Joe Dispenza, in his book *You Are the Placebo*, teaches how powerful beliefs are and how your body transforms when you change your belief.[87]

For beliefs to move beyond behavior modification, a magnified emotion is needed. Emotions are what bind the beliefs in our hearts, good and bad. If you are going to believe differently and think differently, you need to feel differently from your heart.

Magnified Emotions Create Beliefs

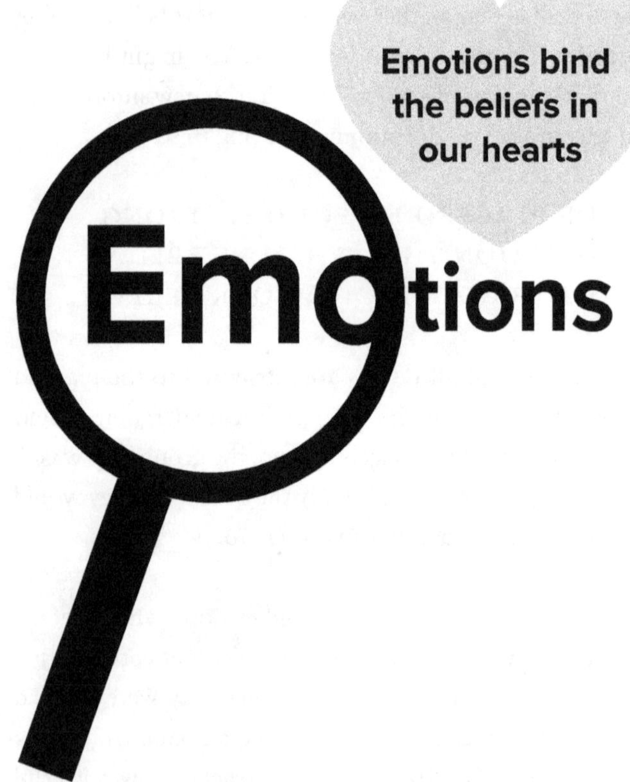

ACTIONS TAKEN IN FAITH

- In your journal, take time to write out "why" you want to advance your career now.
- Decide that you will advance your career no matter what. Send away doubts and fear when they come to your mind because they are not from God.
- Determine what you will have to reprioritize in order to advance your career. You can reflect on your time studying to find the things that are not bringing you joy or allowing you to live at your highest potential.

PRAYER

Dear Heavenly Father, Thank You for equipping me with a powerful mind and the ability to access unlimited potential through faith. Lord, I thank You for bringing me peace through this journey and for strengthening me daily. Lord, I haven't always believed that I was capable and sometimes still have moments of doubt. I know that these things are not from You, Lord, and I ask for Your strength as I grow stronger in my belief. In Jesus' name, Amen.

CHAPTER 12

FAITH THROUGH VISUALIZATIONS

Using a vision board is a great tool to begin the process of raising your frequency by changing your beliefs internally.

I'd heard about vision boards and the process of visualization for years; then a few years ago, for the first time, I created one, and I started to practice visualization regularly. This process opened me up to dreaming about the future and getting clear on the things that I wanted. One of the items I put on my board was winning a John C. Maxwell Culture Award. At the time, I didn't even know what was required to win the award. I just knew that when I saw the award winners that I too wanted to one day earn one of them.

In Chapter 3, we talked about the importance of dreaming. For many of us, we have held ourselves back from dreaming—for a variety of reasons. For some of us, it's not realistic, so what's the point. For others, we forgot how or suppressed our dreaming skills due to our sheer focus on survival. When you are in survival mode, you block your ability to dream of a better life.

By creating a collection of images that express your dreams, you will be able to clearly understand what you are working toward and why it's important.

For me, focusing on this goal meant that I was going to have to grow and get out of my comfort zone. Getting out of that comfort zone meant that I would become a better leader. Being a better leader would impact my family, friends, team, company, clients, and the world around me. This wasn't a probable vision for me to obtain. Each year only eleven awards are given out. There are thousands of people eligible and hundreds of nominations. Each day I would look at my board and complete a meditation in which I would envision myself receiving the award. In addition to my visualizations, I took action to grow daily and to push the limits of what I originally thought possible by dreaming bigger. In 2020, I was presented the "Willfully Grow Award." Before physically receiving this award, I had received it hundreds of times in my mind.

Being clear on the desire and having a vision were the first parts of the process. Additionally, a healthy dose of faith was needed. My likelihood of earning that award, I estimate, was under 1 percent. I had a choice: I could focus on the fact that it would likely not be me or I could focus, with faith, on the possibility that it *would* be me.

Faith is confidence or trust in a person or thing or a belief, without proof.

> HEBREWS 11:1 TELLS US, "NOW FAITH IS CONFIDENCE IN WHAT WE HOPE FOR AND ASSURANCE ABOUT WHAT WE DO NOT SEE."

Faith is different from hope, as hope is an optimistic feeling of expectation for the future. Hope is good, and we want to use hope to stay joyful in our trials. But faith is trusting in the here and now, without knowing what the future will bring.

There's a story in the Bible that tells of Jesus walking on water when His disciples are trapped in a boat during a storm. When the Apostle Peter is scared, Jesus tells him to come out to Him. Peter starts to walk on water, but as he is walking, he takes his focus off Jesus and starts to look at the water and storm around him. When his focus changes, he sinks.[88]

When we are operating from faith, we are focused on God's provision in the midst of our surroundings. But if we focus on our reality over God, we will not live in faith.

The first step to create a vision board is to begin with a clear picture of your heart's desires. You need to look into the future and paint a picture of what you want your life to be like when you have achieved your heart's desires. You have to be able to visualize yourself with clarity living the life you want. This isn't limited to the success you want to achieve in your career. To help you start to form this life, we will create a vision board.

A vision board is a collection of images and words of things that you desire in your life.

Visualization is one of the most powerful mind exercises that you can do. When you visualize, you emit a powerful frequency into the universe. What you put on your board is up to you. Don't worry about how you obtain the items on your vision board. Once you create your board, hang it in your bathroom or above your bed—somewhere you can look at the board every day and then imagine your future self experiencing these things.

Here are some things to include on your vision board:

- Jesus
- Family
- Career goals
- Skills
- Service goals
- Mentors
- Things you want to buy
- Places you want to go
- People you desire relationships with
- Fitness goals
- Ways you want to give back
- Emotions you want to feel
- Experiences

The possibilities are endless.

Don't hold yourself back from putting what you really want on the board. The things that you put on the board don't need to be realistic for your current situation, and most importantly, you don't need the money or a plan to ensure the desired outcome.

Remember, there are no monopolies on dreams, and our God is a mighty God that created you in His image for His purpose. As you create your board, be sure *not to* put things on your board that you don't want. For example, you may desire to be out of debt. If you place the word debt on your board, you will continuously focus your mind on debt. Instead, focus on and write what you do want rather than the debt. This could be a certain amount of money in your bank account or a mock check that you have written out to your favorite charity.

> GOD TELLS US IN PSALMS 37:4, "TAKE DELIGHT IN THE LORD, AND HE WILL GIVE YOU THE DESIRES OF YOUR HEART."

I like to think of my vision board as a picture of my heart's desires. As we take delight and peruse a relationship with the Lord in our hearts, His desires become our desires. God doesn't need a board to know them, but it helps me keep going when I might not feel like it. There is no reason to feel uneasy about anything that you place on the board. God already knows your needs and the intentions in your heart. You won't fool Him by making a board that is incongruent with your heart's desires. But this will cause you to have doubt, and where there is wavering, we cannot receive with faith. Many of the things that have been on my faith board have come to life—from mentors to study under, skills I've gained, to my new convertible.

If this process makes you feel uneasy because you fear that it's materialistic, then take time to explore "why" you want the things on your vision board. Ask yourself, *Do I want these things for selfish reasons, to feel loved, to feel valuable, or to impress others?* If the answer is yes, then take time to pray and ask God to align your heart's desires with His.

When I was growing up, I always wanted to wear clothes that displayed a name brand. I didn't realize this at the time, but I did this because I thought that it made me appear more valuable and important to others. Today, I don't need a label to make me feel valuable or important. I do, however, still want to look good, and there are certain brands that I prefer because of the fit and fabric of the clothing. There is nothing wrong with desiring nice clothing, or anything else for that matter, if your motivations and intentions for it are good. God wants us to enjoy things in life; it's ok to want and have luxury items.

As the months and years pass, you will want to update your board to reflect changes in your life and in your heart. This isn't wishful thinking. It's a powerful act of faith, trusting that God will help you achieve your full potential.

STATEMENT OF FAITH

Next, write out a statement of faith. A statement of faith is also known as a manifesto of your desired future. Like the vision board, don't limit yourself to the things that you can currently figure out how to obtain. A statement of faith is a written document of your desired future. Think as BIG as you want your life to be.

As you write your manifesto, get detailed in your accomplishments, relationships, your faith, position at work, giving, wealth, and lifestyle factors. Your statement of faith needs to include all of the senses and paint a vivid picture of the future.

Manifestos are proven powerful tools to change your life when done correctly. You must take the time to write this down. Over time your manifesto could change as you gain more focus and clarity. But be as clear as you can each step of the way. When we aren't clear, we waste energy. As the old saying goes, "If you chase two rabbits, you won't catch either one."

Sometimes it is challenging for Christians to adopt future beliefs and set goals because they believe that they are trying to control God. God tells us to have the faith of God.

> IN THE GOSPEL OF MARK 9:23, JESUS SAID, "'IF YOU CAN?' EVERYTHING IS POSSIBLE FOR ONE WHO BELIEVES."

Without faith, we doubt God and His ability to give us the desires of our hearts.

You can't manipulate God by expressing your desires. For most of us, we depended on reality to shape our desires instead of trusting God. Psalm 20:4 says, "May he give you the desire of your heart and make all your plans succeed."

Once you write your statement of faith, read it daily for one week before going to bed. Continue to make changes as needed. When you read the statement, you want to visualize yourself in your future life experience feeling all of your senses.

After a week, you can take and store your statement of faith away. If you ever want to come back to it, you can. But it's not required. If you have a spouse or significant other, you can share this with them if you think you can gain from their perspective. But it's perfectly fine for this to be between only you and God.

ACTIONS TAKEN IN FAITH

- Create a vision board.
- Create a Statement of Faith: read it before you go to bed each night for one week.

PRAYER

Dear Heavenly Father, You are El-Roi, The God Who Sees; and Lord, You know the desires of my heart, and You know my needs. Lord, I'm making my plans to prosper, serve, and live abundantly the way You first intended it for me. As I make my plans, Lord, I know that You are already preparing a way. Lord Jesus, give me peace as I take steps forward each day. Give me Your grace and Your strength as a reminder that no matter what the future brings, You are always in control and working things out for my greatest good. Lord Jesus, I have envisioned a future, and I have faith that You will provide it to me, but Lord, I only want this future if it will bring glory to Your name and Kingdom and if it's Your will for me. I give You my life, Lord, and I'm excited for each tomorrow that I'm here to live for You. I ask that You would grant me the desires of my heart, Lord, in Jesus' name. Amen.

CHAPTER 13

CULTIVATING A RELATIONSHIP WITH GOD

What makes a good relationship with God? The same things that make a good relationship with a spouse or friend. When we love someone, we spend time with them, talk to them, listen to them, ask them for help when we need it, help when they need it, and share the same morals and values. That's part of what attracted us to this person in the first place.

The first step in the relationship is to invite God into your heart as your personal Lord and Savior. If you want to put your faith and trust in Jesus today, call on His name. He came to rescue you. Let Him save you today. Call on His name and say this to Him:

Lord Jesus, I know that I'm not perfect, but I believe in You. Come into my heart, save me, and change me. I give You my life. Amen.

God wants us to spend time with Him. He desires us to have a relationship with Him and seek Him first. It's remarkable that looking up, closing your eyes, singing hymns, swaying, and praying all slow down your brainwaves, putting you into a more relaxed state.

There are many ways for us to spend our time with God. There isn't a specific formula that I can give you that will be best for you, but here are things that you can do to meditate with God. These things cannot be done as a ritual to please God, or it's nothing more than intellectual knowledge. If you focus on the ritual or the quantity, you will always feel like you should have done more. Satan will always make you feel like your good isn't good enough.

We can use Jesus as a model for time in prayer. Jesus prayed to His Father, in secret (alone), early in the morning, frequently. He asked for direction, He prayed for others, He prayed with others. Before ministry, after power from the Holy Spirit was released, He prayed with faith and persistence. He prayed from the Bible, and He prayed for God's will.

Praying is the most powerful thing that you can do. Studies have shown that when we pray intentionally with passion in our hearts, we increase the possibility of healing for ourselves and others.[89] Meet God with your heart daily and seek to know Him more than anything else. Start by acknowledging God for the mighty, wonderful Creator that He is by using the many names of God. Acknowledge the promises of God and claim them as your own since you are an heir of Jesus. Then thank Him for the blessings that you have received. Take time to confess, and share with God where you are weak. Then share with Him the desires of your heart. There is no one way to pray. That's the beauty of prayer—as long as the motivation in your heart is to seek a relationship with God and is aligned with God's word, you are praying just fine.

When we don't know how to pray or what to pray for, Paul says in Romans 8:26 that "the Spirit helps us in our weakness. We do not know what we ought to pray for, but the Spirit himself intercedes for us through wordless groans."

Prayer doesn't have to be outwardly apparent. Matthew 6:6 says, "When you pray, go into your room, close the door and pray to your Father, who is unseen. Then your Father, who sees what is done in secret, will reward you." 1 Thessalonians 5:17 tells us to "Never stop praying" (NLT). It doesn't have to be limited by time and space. As you get started with prayer, it's good to have a routine and time set aside. Remember that we have access to the Holy Spirit through prayer at all times.

The Names of God

אבא
Abba
(Father/Daddy)

אהיה
I am
(The Existing One)

אל שהדי
El Shaddai
(Lord God Almighty)

אל עליון
El Elyon
(The Most High God)

אדני
Adonai
(Lord, Master)

יהוה
Yahweh
(Lord, Jehovah)

יהוה נסי
Jehovah Nissi
(The Lord My Banner)

יהוה ראה
Jehovah Raah
(The Lord My Shepherd)

יהוה רפא
Jehovah Rapha
(The Lord That Heals)

יהוה שמה
Jehovah Shammah
(The Lord Is There)

יהוה צדקנו
Jehovah Tsidkenu
(The Lord Our Righteousness)

אלהים
Elohim
(God)

יהוה יראה
Jehovah Jireh
(The Lord Will Provide)

קנא
Qanna
(Jealous)

יהוה מקדשכם
Jehovah Mekoddishkem
(The Lord Who Sanctifies You)

אל עולם
El Olam
(The Everlasting God)

יהוה שלום
Jehovah Shalom
(The Lord Is Peace)

יהוה צבות
Jehovah Sabaoth
(The Lord of Hosts)

If you find yourself having negative thoughts or self-doubt, catch those thoughts, reminding yourself that those thoughts are not from God. Then pray. What's important is that you strengthen your relationship with God and that you turn to God first.

Often when something bad happens at work, we talk to a coworker or spouse first, and when something terrible happens in our lives, we turn to a friend. The truth is God is the One that can fix the problem and help us find the solutions better than anyone else. We must learn to turn to Him first and believe the promises He gives us about the future. We do not know what the future will hold. But we know the One who holds the future.

When we quit looking to the world to solve our problems and start looking for God, we will find peace in our hearts. As a follower of Christ, you cannot depend on what the world tells you is possible based on reality. Your new reality is a life of freedom from your past and a future of peace with God. As it says in the book of Hebrews 11:1, "Faith shows the reality of what we hope for; it is the evidence of things we cannot see" (NLT). Proverbs 3:5–6 tells us to "trust in the LORD with all your heart; do not depend on your own understanding. Seek his will in all you do, and he will show you which path to take" (NLT).

Also, don't forget to pray for your enemies. In the Gospel of Luke 6:27–28, Jesus tells us to "love your enemies, do good to those who hate you, bless those who curse you, pray for those who mistreat you." Maybe there is someone at your workplace that is not supportive or is malicious. Instead of worrying about this person or harboring bitterness toward them, pray to God to come into their hearts and soften them. God will answer our prayers, but we must have faith that He can. When others are against us, God can use what they planned for evil for good. So do not worry; be wise and pray.

RENEWING THE MIND, TAKING THE NEXT STEP

Cultivating a relationship with God is ultimately about having unwavering faith in His promises and experiencing them as our reality. When you have an abiding awareness of Christ in you, and operate your life based off what He says is true, then you move into flow with Him. At this point, you will no longer need to operate relying solely on your senses or your past experiences. This leads to incredible peace and confidence, not in ourselves, but in what God can do for us and through us.

> IN MATTHEW 22:37, JESUS SAID "YOU SHALL LOVE THE LORD YOUR GOD WITH ALL YOUR HEART, AND WITH ALL YOUR SOUL, AND WITH ALL YOUR MIND" (ESV).

All of the exercises provided will help you create new thoughts, beliefs, and allow you to live with more energy than you currently do. To renew our minds, we must commit to the process until it works. Your method for connecting with God and manifesting your future may look different than others. There is no one right way to have a relationship with God.

It is easier for some people than for others to override the subconscious mind shaped by our environment. If you doubt or waiver, it can slow the speed at which your mind is renewed. We must continually seek God, stay rooted in His Word, and find areas of our lives that are not aligned with God's will.

We are no less righteous to God because we are sinners and

have doubt. But our inability to see ourselves the way God sees us stops us from taking the actions required for us to have the life we desire.

To renew our minds, we can read scripture, evaluate our life, and reconcile where we are off track. This is not a self-judgment process, although many people lose sight of the benefit because they continue to condemn themselves for the past. When you can identify an area of your life that is not in line with what God says, you can ask for forgiveness, forgive yourself, and pray for God's grace as you move forward in life.

Our minds are naturally good at recalling our past faults, failures, shortcomings, pains, and mistakes. This is not how God created you, and it's not what He sees when He looks at you. God doesn't see a single blemish or flaw. In His eyes, you are perfectly crafted in every way. He sees the best in you, He sees your highest potential, and He loves you the way you are.

The more we gain wisdom and an understanding of who God says we are, the more we can understand that we have infinite potential. God is love. He is the purest form of love. There isn't a single person that He creates of lesser quality or value than another.

The world equates and places value on people because of their ability, gender, race, social-economic class, appearance, voice, talents, and possessions. There are countless standards that we are supposed to live up to in order to be seen as acceptable and valuable. In God's eyes, you can never be more valuable and perfect than you are right now because it's not you that earns your value. Our value comes from God's love and grace that is freely given; we are perfectly and wonderfully made. Psalm

139:13–14 says, "For you created my inmost being; you knit me together in my mother's womb. I praise you because I am fearfully and wonderfully made; your works are wonderful, I know that full well."

Many Christians do not understand that they are connected to the ultimate power source of God's grace. God's grace is His ability. This is the same power that Jesus used to perform the miracles in the Bible. Jesus didn't perform the miracles as God. He performed the miracles as a man through the power of the Holy Spirit. Jesus lives in us, and we are heirs to His inheritance, and because He is in us, we have the same access to grace. That means that we do not have to depend on the known and the seen in the world. We are plugged into God's grace. Ephesians 2:8–10 says, "For by grace you have been saved through faith. And this is not your own doing; it is the gift of God, not a result of works, so that no one may boast. For we are his workmanship, created in Christ Jesus for good works, which God prepared beforehand, that we should walk in them" (ESV).

To use God's grace (God's ability), we cannot depend on our ability. We must surrender and let God work through us. When the good work is completed, we must thank the Lord and humbly give God credit. To surrender, we must admit that we cannot do this alone and that we want grace to work. Paul tells us in Romans 12:2, "Do not conform to the pattern of this world, but be transformed by the renewing of your mind. Then you will be able to test and approve what God's will is—his good, pleasing and perfect will." The renewal of our minds comes when we surrender to Jesus; this is where we will find peace, joy, love, and grace.

Non-believers do not have access to this power because, without Jesus, the power source is missing. When we are working only as human beings, then the weight of the world is on our shoulders; it's up to us to have the knowledge and strength to figure everything out. We are responsible for every outcome and often try to control everything and everyone around us. It works, to some extent, but it destroys a person's life because there is little balance, large amounts of stress, and our desire for more is never enough. The driving force is accomplishments, position, power, and money—leading to fear, overwhelm, burnout, and hopelessness.

The way that God works won't always be logical to us. We cannot predict and determine how we will get the desires of our hearts. We must remain faithful, thankful, and surrender to the will of God. If we hold on tight to what we have today, we can't be ready to receive all God has planned for us. We must be willing to give everything that we have received with a joyful heart—never trying to manufacture something out of God but continuously pursuing a relationship with Him out of love.

In our hearts, we must be ok with everything we have acquired in this life to be taken away, knowing that we are deeply loved and valued by God no matter what possessions or titles we have. Letting go isn't always a physical giving away of things. God wants us to be prosperous and to enjoy life. That's why He gave Adam and Eve everything they needed in the first place.[90]

Of course, sin weighs our hearts and minds down, straining our relationship with God. It's not that God loves us any less or sees us any differently when we sin. Sin drives us to hide from God. The ways of the flesh are sinful. Sin allures us by telling us that it will bring us pleasure, and at the moment, it can bring a small amount of pleasure, but sin always has a consequence. It's not that God punishes us or that Satan attacks us. Ultimately it is our choices that most often cause our pain.

Side note: If you are in an emotionally or physically abusive relationship currently or were in the past, I'm not saying that you chose the abuse or that you are choosing it. I pray that you escape. I, too, have been in abusive relationships, and leaving isn't an easy thing to do. Most often, we are made to believe that we are nothing, that we won't survive without the other person, and if we do leave, that we are responsible for the other person hurting themselves. Sometimes we are held by fear of physical pain to ourselves and our family.

The same was true for Jesus. Jesus had the same temptations that man has because He was fully man. To help Him work through the temptations of sin, Jesus used God's grace (ability). You can do the same thing. God can help you. But you must ask for help and believe that He is helping you.[91]

When we try to advance in our careers, we can fall into temptation and sin if we are not careful. I know that I did, instead of fearing the Lord and turning to Him. I feared my manager, and therefore I did what he asked me to do. He asked me to do some things that weren't in alignment with what God wants me to do. I was so caught up in trying to please him and so afraid of getting fired that I would morph my character into whatever was needed at the moment.

This experience taught me to always hold true to my values and principles.

It took me years to get out of this place and take a stand for myself. Those years were painful and caused great strain on my marriage, my children, my friendships, and they drove me further away from God. This was a choice I made.

If you have areas of sin in your life, ask God to help you and believe that He will. It's not that you need to try and live a perfect life. You don't need to condemn yourself when you slip up. Ask for forgiveness, and then forgive yourself. You were born a sinner, but the more you can stay out of sin, the more significant relationship you can have with the Lord because you will not try to hide from Him. The more you are connected, the more wisdom you will gain.

If you take the next step with faith, God can give you far more than you ever thought possible. When we listen for God in our hearts, we will start to hear Him. All that we have to do is be willing to take the next step. You cannot fully step into the life that God has for you if you are unwilling to take the next step without knowing the next step.

Many times you will not know what the next step is until you take the first step. God isn't going to guide you into a place where He is not willing to help you. It doesn't matter if you don't possess a particular skill or lack experience. You have to trust God to take you to your next step in your career.[92]

The same way that David, the shepherd boy, had to be willing to stand up to Goliath. David wasn't the biggest, the strongest, the most qualified fighter, but He was chosen by God and had His favor.[93] You have God's favor, too, and no matter what may seem impossible to you in your career and life is possible through God.[94]

To receive what God wants you to have in your life, you have to take action. James 2:17 tells us, "Faith by itself, if it is not accompanied by action, is dead." When we believe or have faith, then our actions will align with our beliefs. We cannot expect that God will motivate us to take the next step in our career.

God simply guides us through, and when we take the steps, He is there to help us.

YOU HAVE TO TAKE THE STEP IN FAITH THAT GOD WILL BE WITH YOU.

If you want to advance in your career, you need to talk to your manager about it. In the remainder of the book, you will learn how to build a promotion plan to showcase your work and ideas. Reading the book will help you write a promotion plan and approach your manager. But what you do with that knowledge is up to you. If you write your plan but don't talk to your manager, you're not walking in faith. God can only provide you with His grace when you are taking action.

Before each promotion plan, I prayed a lot.

I didn't have a crystal ball to tell me how the promotion plan would turn out. In fact, I was nervous the day that I turned my first one in. So nervous that I slipped it on my manager's desk. I knew that if I wouldn't have taken that action, then I wouldn't have been promoted. To my delight, my manager was so impressed with the plan that he came to my door and asked when we would meet to talk about my ideas.

God can and will help you if you ask and take action. If we gain knowledge and take no action, it only leads us to frustration and more self-doubt. When we need to get more and more information before we take a single step, we are not living in faith and grace. Faith says I am willing to take the next step because my success depends not on my knowledge and ability but on the God of the universe that I am fully surrendered to.

Being surrendered to God and living in faith doesn't mean that everything will be perfect and without work. There will be times when things don't go the way that we planned them to go. We cannot see these things as failures. When our plans don't work out, we should examine our motives and intentions to ensure that they are pure, and if they are, then all that's required to do is praise God. Praising God in our trials helps us to remain connected and in peace.[95]

When we are continually seeking the Kingdom of God, we will find peace in our trials, knowing that God has something greater in store for us. Sometimes we don't dream big enough for ourselves, and God helps us to avoid mistakes.

The world will never see you the way that God sees you. You can expect that people will point out your shortcomings, imperfections, and won't always want you to succeed. When this happens, we must not take these things to heart, writing limitations on our life. Instead, we should reject the thoughts and remember that we are righteous in the eyes of God. No one can make you think less of yourself, even if they think less of you. You are now in the driver's seat of your thoughts, words, and actions.

Many people live in a constant state of fear, worry, and anxiety because they remain stuck in the faults of their past, depend on their own ability for the future, and cannot see past their current reality. You, my beautiful friend in Christ Jesus, are no longer one of these people. As you daily seek God's Kingdom and to love others, you will find it.

Jesus at the Root

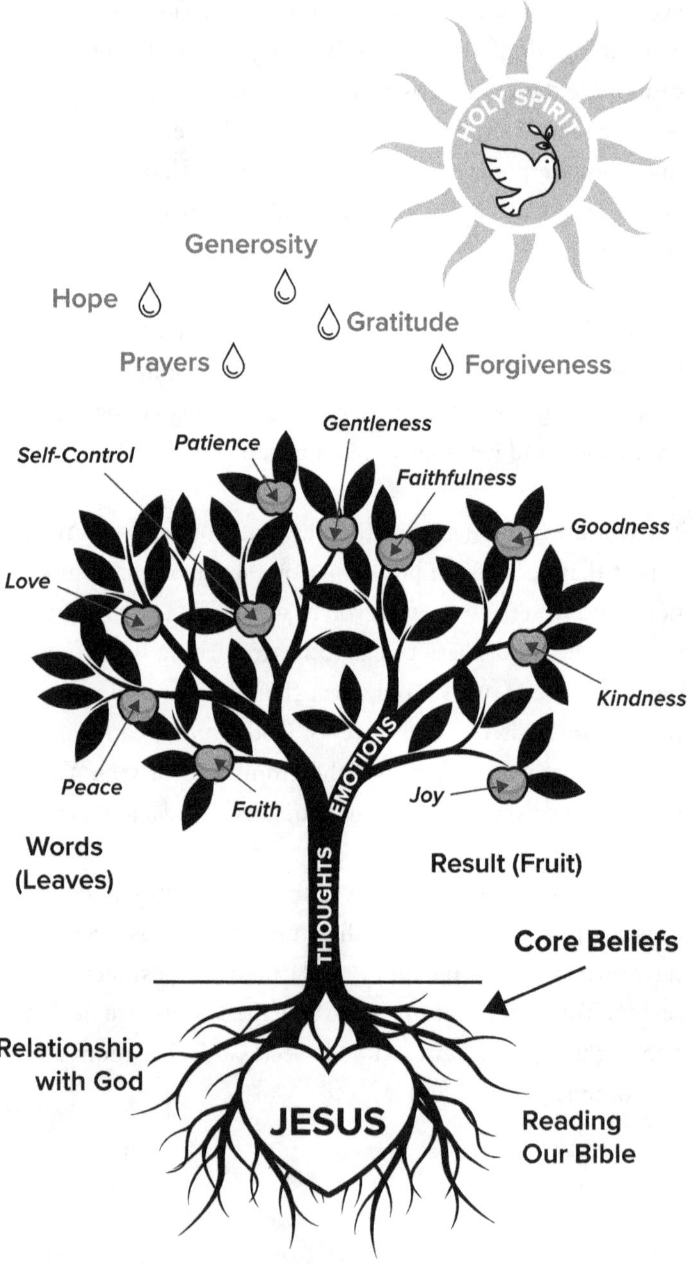

As Jesus said in Matthew 7:7, "Ask and it will be given to you; seek and you will find; knock and the door will be opened to you."

Every prayer thought, word, intention, and action instantly impact our energy and the world. Choose to love God, love yourself, and love others as yourself today.

MINDFULNESS, MEDITATION, AND VISUALIZATION

I was raised a Catholic, and other than saying repetitive prayers at meals and bedtime, religion was a thing that happened on Sunday. So when I thought of meditation, I didn't understand that this was something that God instructed us to do.

But what does God say about meditation?

The words "meditate" and "meditation" occur in the Bible twenty-three times.

TO MEDITATE MEANS TO THINK DEEPLY OR CAREFULLY ABOUT SOMETHING

Remember when we were talking about those negative thoughts before? That was a form of meditation, but it wasn't a positive one.

When we meditate in a positive way, we can reduce the stress that is built up in our bodies. If we think of ourselves as a glass, there is a limited amount of space in the glass. In our lives we have stress which can be represented by water, and over time our glass gets fuller and fuller, and unless we remove water from the glass, we become overloaded with stress. Although our bodies can process and remove stress, it can only happen at a certain rate. Too much stress affects every area of our lives and causes us to be out of balance because our bodies cannot naturally process and remove the stress. Something as simple as a twenty-minute meditation can help your body process the same amount of stress that would normally take you hours of sleeping to remove.[96]

To enter into a meditative state, you start with mindfulness. Mindfulness is simply having awareness of your body and being fully present in the moment. So often, we live in the past or the future when instead, we could teach ourselves to live in the present. As a result, we can experience more happy and fulfilling lives.

Once you are present and in the relaxed alpha state, it's the perfect time to bring in visualization. When we visualize things, our bodies and brains experience them as being real—meaning that they have already happened according to our mind, and because we have had these experiences, new neural pathways are created in your brain. Your brain literally cannot distinguish between something you have experienced and something that you have visualized experiencing. By adding your senses and details to your visualization, you make the neural pathways even stronger. The more time you spend meditating, the stronger the pathways get. Additionally, when you stop having the repeated thoughts of doubt, worry, and negativity, those neural pathways weaken.

Neural Pathways

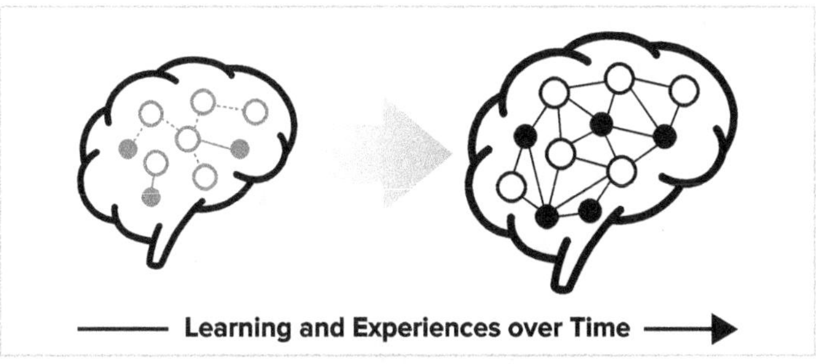

How the Brain Changes

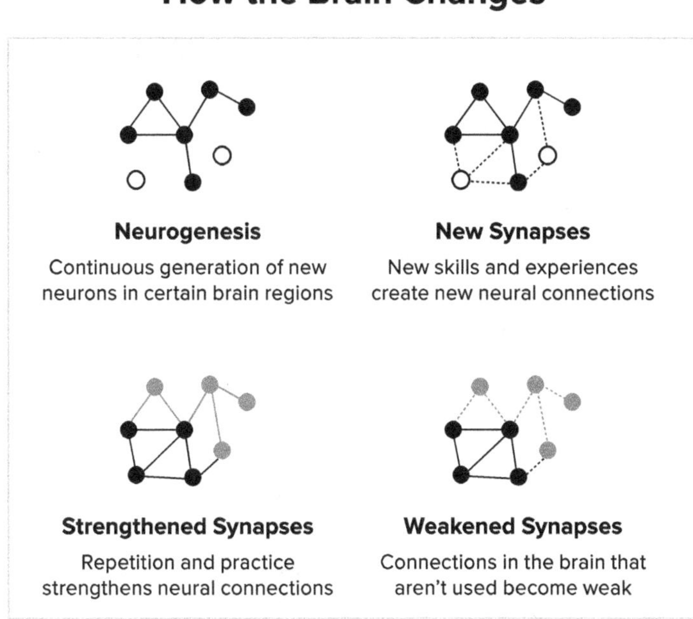

As your neural pathways form, you will start to change the way you think about your abilities to achieve the things that you want in life, allowing you to more easily take the actions required to live the life that you desire, because now your body and mind believe that you are capable. By adding in mindfulness, meditation, and visualization, you will be able to remove the layers of stress, allowing you to experience peace during times that historically would have brought you overwhelming amounts of stress.

Here's a simple meditation outline.

1. Find a quiet place with a comfortable seat. This might be a chair or a couch, or wherever you'd like, so long as you're able to sit upright with your feet on the floor uncrossed. Try to find a chair where your head is not supported; this will aid you in not falling asleep. Laying down is ok, but not generally recommended since people fall asleep. Place your hands in your lap or on your side as long as they do not touch each other. If you want to have soft spa-like music in the background, you can, or playing a track by Berry Goldstein will help you to relax further.
2. Take a moment to look up with your eyes at a spot on the wall close to the ceiling without tilting your head up. Close your eyes. Breath slowly and deeply in and out through your nose. Then another. With each exhale, let your muscles soften a little further.
3. Continue to breath slowly, and take a moment to settle where you are. Bring awareness by involving your senses, but release all judgement. Take a few minutes to scan your entire body and release all of the tension from your body.
4. To relax even further, imagine that you are going down a staircase with a railing, and count backward from ten to one, allowing yourself to go down slowly; with each step, relax even deeper.
5. When you reach the bottom of the staircase, imagine a door, and as you open the door, you enter a secret place where you will take time to commune with God. Your secret place can be any place that you feel comfortable—be it a beach, meadow, mountain, or any other place.
6. While in your secret place, you may meet Jesus and talk to Him, or you may meditate and think about a name of God, a promise of God, a single word, Bible verse, or phrase. Take time to think about and experience with as many senses as possible what God says is true for

you today. For example, if you meditate on Isaiah 41:10 ("So do not fear, for I am with you; do not be dismayed, for I am your God. I will strengthen you and help you; I will uphold you with my righteous right hand"), then you will want to imagine yourself today living out this promise. Maybe there are times when you are typically afraid or feel weakened. Rather than visualizing and meditating on you feeling weak and discouraged, take time to imagine yourself in those same situations, but with the strength of God. What would you do, think, and feel if you were living a life of freedom the way that God intended it?

7. At the end of your time, start to bring yourself back to awareness by counting up slowly from one to five, becoming more and more awake and aware with each number. As you become more aware, start to gently wiggle your fingers and toes. (You can alternate the ending to say you are going into a deep sleep if you are completing this meditation before bed.)

Note: The meditation can be as short as fifteen minutes, or you can go for longer if you like. It's important to be consistent to get results. It's equally important not to condemn yourself if you miss a meditation. If you miss meditating in the morning, then try a day meditation or one before bed, remembering that the more you do the meditations and visualizations, the more powerful the effects will be. At first, you may not feel like it's working. That's just your subconscious mind trying to fight you, and it's part of the process for many people.

REVERSING STUCK LIMITING BELIEFS

Everything that we have covered up to this point will help you renew your mind, with Jesus deep within your heart. A renewed mind will give you peace. But that doesn't mean we won't experience roadblocks or conflicts that get in the way of the new beliefs we are trying to adopt. If you have been completing your Actions Taken in Faith daily and it feels like something is incongruent, or you desire to increase the speed of harmonizing your heart, then you may need additional support to adopt a new belief more quickly.

Stress from conflicting thoughts and feelings (fear, doubt, worry, anger, anxiety) can get stuck in your body and make it harder for you to adopt your new beliefs.

To fast-track my renewed mind, I've used three tools. These are merely tools that help the body function at the level God intended for it to by clearing trapped energy and ensuring that your natural energy centers are open and clear. These are not spiritual practices and shouldn't be taken as such. These are merely tools that work with the laws that God used to create us and the universe. When we talked previously about the ability to change beliefs, we talked about tapping into the subconscious mind by getting in the theta state (I Am affirmations, daily meditation and visualization, and prayer), repetition (learning how to type), and having a magnified emotion (like when I went to Vegas). These tools created a magnified experience that rapidly releases and reprograms the body and mind when done in conjunction with your daily faith actions.[97]

RELEASE TRAPPED EMOTIONS

The first tool is to release trapped emotions. I first learned about releasing trapped emotions through Dr. Jim Richards's Heart Physics® Coach Certification training.[98] This is in alignment with Dr. Bradley Nelson's "Emotion Code" techniques.[99] Both practitioners teach about the potential of trapped emotions in your body. Emotions can be inherited for generations or in your lifetime and trapped like a ball of energy resonating at a lower frequency inside you. This trapped frequency over time will cause that area of the body to become weaker and subsequently prone to injury or disease. Because our bodies' energy and frequencies naturally resonate with each other, the trapped emotion will start to affect other tissues and organs in the body.

To locate trapped emotions, applied kinesiology, or muscle testing, is used to show the body's reaction in the weakening or strengthening of its muscles in response to a thought or a question. This technique helps us get "yes" or "no" answers from the body, and we use it to get information about imbalances that are causing emotional or physical problems. This works because all the information about our bodies is stored in the subconscious mind. Once a trapped emotion is identified, we are able to delete or release it using a magnet by running it over the energy line in the body called the governing meridian. This can be likened to taking a credit card and running it over a magnet; the magnet changes or deletes the information on the card. In the same way, once we have identified a trapped emotion (by accessing the info from the subconscious mind using applied kinesiology), we run the magnet over the governing meridian, and this deletes or releases the energy from the body.

CAUTION ABOUT MAGNETS

Magnets are generally considered quite safe, but there are a few occasions when they should not be used, or should only be used after they have been approved by a physician, including during pregnancy and the use of implanted pumps for insulin or pain relief, cochlear implants, pacemakers, shunts for the treatment of hydrocephalus (which sometimes are adjusted by magnets), and MAGEC rods used for children to correct severe scoliosis, which are also adjusted by magnets.

From a distance, a trained practitioner is able to run the magnet over themselves, as they have permission to be a proxy for the client, and this releases the trapped emotion from the client. After the emotion is released, the client creates an affirmation of their new belief to repeat for a few days. After learning this technique, I used it on myself to release trapped emotions that were holding me back from living at my highest potential. I've worked on all sorts of things with a trained practitioner, and after the sessions I could feel less resistance toward the things I wanted to change. This has improved my confidence, relationships, and enhanced my ability to feel at peace in my own skin. I recommend this technique to my clients when they are feeling particularly challenged in an area or have resistance in taking action. Emotions can become trapped for any number of reasons, and although we may feel that we have moved on, dissident frequencies can remain.

EMOTIONAL FREEDOM TECHNIQUE

The second tool is the Emotional Freedom Technique (EFT). Gary Craig discovered EFT, which is meridian-based therapy similar to acupuncture, but no needles are used. Instead, the client taps on various acupuncture points on the client's face, body, and hands, while the client focuses on the issue that needs to be healed by repeating phrases about it. For example, "Fearful of talking about money" or "pain in my right knee." EFT has been shown to reduce anxiety, depression, stress, pain, PTSD, aid weight loss, and other things.[100] I've used EFT with family members to help them reduce pain and during emotional times. With clients, we use EFT to help build confidence and reduce nerves through the career advancement process. Each time it has helped the person's pain and stress level come down. What's great about EFT is it's fast and easy to do.

REPENTANCE

The third tool is repentance.

> **THE WORD REPENT IN THE BIBLE MEANS TO CHANGE DIRECTION.**

If we have faulty core beliefs, unforgiveness, bitterness, resentment, guilt, or shame, then it will hold us back from living the life that God wants us to. The book of Proverbs and the four books of the Gospel have been great resources to prepare my heart for repentance. I've found that the Amplified Bible is the easiest to comprehend, but you can use any version that you prefer.

As we continue our walk with the Lord, we will understand more and more of what God is saying to us because our heart is fertile soil. As you walk through Proverbs, write the verses about communication and foolishness. Evaluate each Proverb, and if you are not acting accordingly, then write down the verse. Then pray for repentance. Next, write down how you will operate in accordance with the verse.

In the Gospel, study how Jesus lived. Write down anytime that He prays, how He treats people, how He uses faith.

Reflect on your life and repent if needed. Thank God for giving us the living example of how He wants us to live our lives. When we follow God's plan in the Bible, our lives become more peaceful. Challenges don't go away, but we are better able to handle the challenges. You will start to notice the fruit of your labor quickly as you study God's word. He will be filling your heart. Others may not see you changing, but be patient with yourself. It took me about nine months of practicing the mindset work consistently for my family to notice a difference. I'm still me, but now I don't react the same way to life. I no longer have unexplainable rages of anger, and when in a stressful situation, I nearly always immediately turn to God in prayer, and the stress is reduced. With these tools, you too can more effectively and efficiently renew your mind and enjoy lasting peace.

Each of the tools that you have been provided with are incredible and make harmonizing the heart and renewing the mind easier. What's great is that these tools work quickly, are noninvasive, and have no long-term negative side effects. All of the methods can be learned quickly and performed on yourself if you so choose. No matter your decision to work with a trained practitioner or try the methods yourself, I hope you will have an open mind to these new tools that can provide rapid changes. We must not only depend on the things that we can see when we work to correct the unseen. Our not seeing gravity or radio waves doesn't make them any less real or powerful. When we can remove stress and improve our energy, then our body can more easily naturally heal itself. One amazing side effect that I've personally experienced is the removal of my shoulder pain that I had and treated for over a decade. I tried everything from chiropractors, lifting weights, pain meds, muscle relaxers, X-rays, massages, acupuncture, supplements, foam rolling, stretching, and muscle rubs—to no avail. Everything that I tried only provided temporary relief and never got to the root of my problem. Today, I live pain-free, and just like I could never explain what happened to cause the pain, I do not know what caused it to go away, but I do believe that it went away because my body is operating the way that God intended it to. To me this is the miracle I've been praying for, for so many years.

ACTIONS TAKEN IN FAITH

- Take time to reflect on how renewing your mind is going.
- Check out the bonus videos and more detailed information on using the three tools listed in this chapter by going to www.GodsNotDoneWithYouBook.com/bonus. All of these tools you can learn to do on your own, or you can work with a trained practitioner to save additional time.
- Schedule time daily to go on a date with God, to feed your soul by reading your Bible.
- Start your day with prayer before your feet hit the ground.
- Commit to praying first if you become discouraged or feel challenged.
- Pray continually and surrender to God's grace in everything you do.
- Set alarms throughout the day to pray.
- Keep a journal with prayers and things God speaks to you. Record the times that God answered your prayers.
- Write a commitment to God in your journal that you will take the actions required with faith to advance your career and live out His will no matter what your feelings are.
- Take time for meditation at least one time per day. It's important to be consistent. You will want to meditate first thing in the morning after getting out of bed. Don't drink anything other than water. Your body is naturally in a theta state, and this will make your meditation easier.

PRAYER

Dear Heavenly Father, You are Jehovah-Bore, the Lord, my Creator, and I thank You for creating my energy systems so intercurrently and for showing me new tools that can help me to raise my frequency. I ask that You help me to know the right tools for me to raise my energy to the highest levels to remove all pain and bring my body and my heart frequency back to the original frequency that You intended for me. Lord, I'm so grateful for You and the laws that You put into place when You created the universe. I ask that You help me to identify and overcome the things that are subconsciously holding me back from advancing in my career. Let my power be restored so that I can be clear and renewed so that the invisible walls that have caused me resistance would be shattered once and for all. Give me Your grace to avoid things that are not good for my body. Lord, I pray that Your loving energy fills every cell in my body, heart, and mind so that I can experience the peace that surpasses all understanding and be a model of Your grace and love to the world. In Jesus' name, Amen.

CHAPTER 14

CIRCLE OF INFLUENCE

As our thoughts and beliefs influence our lives, the same is true for the attitudes and beliefs of people we spend time with.

PROVERBS 27:17 TELLS US THAT "AS IRON SHARPENS IRON, SO ONE PERSON SHARPENS ANOTHER."

Too often in our workplaces, we see the opposite: people make themselves less productive and appear to achieve less, all for the sake of being liked and fitting in.

I once had a friend call me and ask me if she should quit getting so much done at work because it made a couple of her coworkers feel uncomfortable. She feared that her success would make them look bad.

This is one of the worst things that you can do for your career. Yes, you need to get along with people at work and work as a team, but you never want to diminish your abilities because it makes others uncomfortable. You own who you are as an employee for your entire life. It directly affects your ability to earn promotions and raises. And remembering that our work is an act of worship, we should never limit what God wants to do through us.

Whom we spend our time with has a direct impact on our faith, thinking, energy, and careers. If you take a look at the five people you spend the most time with and average their incomes, it will be close to what you are making today.

You want to continually surround yourself with people who know more than you do and have achieved higher success levels than you have. Equally important are the attitudes and thoughts of the people around you. If the people you hang out with are not driven, have negative thoughts, and dwell in fear, they will take you down with them. Paul tells us in 1 Corinthians 15:33, "Do not be misled: 'Bad company corrupts good character.'"

Jesus had a clear circle of influence in His twelve disciples, Mary Magdalene, and His family. Although no one could be higher or greater than Jesus, the people who were in His daily circle had many things in common. They loved and supported Jesus, they believed that He was the Messiah, and they helped Him complete God's Will for Him here on Earth. Additionally, they were each uniquely gifted and helped Jesus' ministry accordingly.

Write down the names of the five people you spend the most time with, either in person or on the phone, who aren't your adolescent kids. If you have a spouse, include them on your list.

For the next five statements, consider each person on your list and put a plus for each person that fits the criteria below. If they don't fit the criteria, then put a minus.

1. This person speaks positively when I share my thoughts and ideas.
2. This person speaks positively about their work and life.
3. This person doesn't make me feel bad when I make mistakes or am vulnerable with them.
4. This person has the same spiritual beliefs as I do or makes decisions in the same moral way.
5. This person sets high goals and is growing or is in a higher position than you at work, or they earn more than you, or they have accomplished something that you haven't and want to.

Now take a look at your list. How many people have five plus marks? Do you have any? Four? Anyone with three or fewer is not serving you well in your inner circle.

When we find people who are not serving our lives positively, we need to adjust our inner circle. For some people, that is letting someone go in your life. This is a hard thing to do.

LOSING PEOPLE IS HARD, BUT STAYING STUCK BECAUSE OF OTHERS IS WORSE.

Some people you may not be able to remove from your life, but you can limit the amount of time you spend with them.

When you start building your promotion plan, which we'll be going over soon, I want you to be able to share it with your inner circle. But if a person is negative, do not share this promotion plan experience with them until after submitting your plan and earning your raise or promotion.

Whenever we try something new to better our lives, it's not uncommon for others to doubt us. They might tell us it won't work, along with many other discouraging and crazy things. People who do this are not helping you reach your goals. They likely think that they are helping you by bringing you back to reality, but in fact, they are keeping you stuck in *their* reality. Deep down, they are not confident in who they are. Confident people help others in positive ways.

Have you ever tried to eat healthier only to have a "friend" buy you a dessert or pressure you to splurge? Or maybe they simply made rude comments about your diet. If so, they're sabotaging you. Don't enlist them in your promotion plan process; it will only bring you down. Look out for this type of behavior, and only share with the people who support you.

What should you do if your husband doesn't meet the criteria? Panic and get rid of him. Just kidding—you don't need to go ditching your husband or turn to panic. Even better news: you don't need to try and change your husband. What I've found to work best at influencing everyone around me, especially my husband, is working on myself without expecting anything in return. Praying for your husband is another good tool.

But what if your husband doesn't support you in advancing your career? This is a really hard one, ladies, and I wish that it was black and white, but there is a lot of gray. When our husbands are not supportive, it can cause a lot of stress and resistance. Before making a decision on what to do, consider what type of husband you have. First of all, if your husband is a God-fearing, devoted Christian, that is, surrendering to the Lord as he leads your family, then maybe God is telling Him that there is something different your family needs right now. If your husband is not in a relationship with God and surrendering to Him to lead the family, then you need to consult with God on what you are supposed to do. Oftentimes, when our husbands don't want us to do something, it's out of love and protection for you and the family. Take time to talk to your husband about wanting to advance your career, and listen to his concerns. It won't be uncommon for your husband to have beliefs about women working based on his childhood and what his mother did. No matter the situation, ask God to help you address it with your husband.

Here are three ways that you can build a stronger circle of influence.

First, look inside your company. Who is successful and made the journey you want to make. To become closer to this person, you can take them to lunch, enlist them as a mentor, take an interest in their work, offer to help them with their work or projects, or ask them to train you in a specific area. Asking others for advice makes them feel good, and they want the advice they gave you to work out. Respect them by listening, following through, and being prepared with what you want to learn when you sit down.

The second way to upgrade your circle of influence is to get into mastermind groups with others. A mastermind is a group of people that come together with a common mission or interest. It's great to be in a group with people who have diverse backgrounds and experiences. Masterminds allow you time to work on yourself, your company, and the opportunity to learn from others. As you continue to move up, it's not uncommon for your company to pay for you to be in a mastermind. We will cover this more in Chapter 24 when you build a personal development and growth plan.

The third way to upgrade your circle of influence is to find a group or mentor at church. Check with your local congregation to see if they have any groups for career women or women in leadership. If your church doesn't have any, you can check with other local churches.

Share the career advancement journey you are embarking on with three people. Take time to write down in your journal and commit to the three people you will share it with. These people can help to be your accountability partners. Having a partner makes us show up even when we may not feel like it.

ACTIONS TAKEN IN FAITH

- Evaluate your circle of influence.
- Upgrade your circle of influence as needed.
- If you can't think of three people or want additional accountability partners, join our leadership and accountability group at www.GodsNotDoneWithYouBook.com/bonus.

PRAYER

Dear Heavenly Father, You are Jehovah-Roi, my Shepard, the Wisest, and are filled with goodness. Lord, help me to see who You would want me to have in my closest circle and whom I should be spending the most time with, in order to do Your will here on Earth. Help me reduce the time that I have in relationships that diminish my confidence in Your plans for me. And when I do spend time with those that are not speaking life into me, cover me with a blanket of protection as to not let their words, actions, and energy affect me. Lord, give me Your strength to be a greater friend and to encourage those that spend their time with me. Lord, help me to connect with others that are going to bring me closer to You and that will plant seeds of hope and encouragement within me. I thank You for allowing me to make new connections that will continue to lift up my spirit as I advance in my career and grow in my walk with You. I love You, Lord Jesus. Amen.

Part 3

TRANSFORMING YOUR CAREER

In Part 2, we covered everything you need to harmonize your heart and renew your mind. As we move into Part 3, I want you to continue to stay focused daily on renewing your mind until it becomes a habit.

They say that it takes twenty-one days to create a new habit. I've seen it work, and I've seen it not work. Here's what I'll say at first when you try to implement everything you've learned: your body will be fighting you. Your body is not in charge; remember you control your thoughts, and you control your body. Don't listen to your feelings for the first ninety days if they are telling you not to do the work. Do it anyway. After ninety days, you will be more ingrained in your habits, but don't stop. Satan wants nothing more than for you to quit spending time with God and to live in misery. Don't let him win this battle. God wants nothing more than a relationship with you. Make it a mission to be best friends with God for life.

In Part 3, we now turn our focus to building your promotion plan and transforming your career. As we go through each part of the promotion plan, the actions you need to take will be found in the Building Your Plan recap at the end of each chapter. You will be given the number of days and amount of time recommended to complete them. Using this guide, you can complete your plan in thirty days while giving yourself enough time and space to fully develop your ideas while still having time to complete your Daily Mind Renewal Routine. As you go through the chapters, I recommend that you complete each step as you go; this will save you time as you will not need to reread the chapters, and it will help you to avoid procrastination and increase motivation. By taking daily consistent steps, your plan will develop over time, and before you know it, you will be in your manager's office talking about the future of your career.

To make it easier, I've put together a Daily Mind Renewal Routine, a 30-Day Journal, and a 30-Day No-Fail Plan that you can download at www.GodsNotDoneWithYouBook.com/bonus.

Daily Mind Renewal Routine

Date: ____________

Body

☐ Hydrate ___ 8 ___ 8 ___ 4 ___ 2	☐ Move your body ______ mins	☐ Grounding ____ mins (use a mat or go barefoot outside)

Mind

☐ Meditation and visualization upon waking

☐ Surround yourself with positive people

Affirmations

☐ AM ☐ Noon ☐ PM

I am

____

____

____

____

____

Speak & Think *Life*	I passed on judgement and got *Curious* when...
☐ Myself ☐ Spouse, Significant Other, Future Relationship ☐ Family ☐ Friends ☐ Dreams	

GOD'S NOT DONE WITH YOU - DAILY MIND RENEWAL ROUTINE | MARY E. GUIROVICH

My career goal:

Today's 3 Wins
1. ______
2. ______
3. ______

Next 5 Priorities
1. ______
2. ______
3. ______
4. ______
5. ______

Spirit

Bible Reading/Reflection	Gratitude

Prayer

I prayed:	My Prayers	Prayers Answered
☐ Upon Waking ☐ To Surrender ☐ For Grace ☐ For Strength ☐ Before Becoming Discouraged ☐ Without Ceasing ☐ ______		

30-Day No Fail Plan

Building Your Plan

	Create Your CAJ
Days 1–2	○ ○
	1 hour per day
	Write Your Appreciation Letter
Days 3–4	○ ○
	1 hour per day
	Owning Your Accomplishments
Days 5–7	○ ○ ○
	1 hour per day
	Adding Value Through New Ideas
Days 8–13	○ ○ ○ ○ ○ ○
	1 hour per day
	Personal Development and Growth Plan
Days 14–16	○ ○ ○
	2 hours per day
	Salary Research
Day 17	○
	1 hour per day
	Closing and Polishing Your Plan
Days 18–22	○ ○ ○ ○ ○
	1 hour per day
	Preparing For Your Meeting
Days 23–26	○ ○ ○ ○
	2 hours per day

Plus 4 Days of Rest of Your Choice

CHAPTER 15

HOW NOT TO ASK FOR A PROMOTION

Thomas Edison once said, "I have not failed. I've just found ten thousand ways that won't work."

A common mistake in career advancement is asking for a promotion in the wrong way. I've made many mistakes myself, and seen it happen to others. Before we move into how to create your promotion plan, it's important to understand what doesn't work.

This chapter will not only teach you how not to ask for a promotion, but why you may have asked and failed in the past. That doesn't mean that you are a failure or incapable of achieving a promotion or raise. It means that you need to change your approach.

Let's briefly look at the mistakes people make when trying to advance their careers, and then we will talk about how to do it the right way and avoid the mistakes.

First and foremost, if you are not a good employee, it will be hard to earn raises and promotions in general. It's possible, but not probable. So being an excellent employee that arrives early, has a positive attitude, completes their work, and cheerfully steps up to help others is the first step. Many women work harder and are more productive than men.[101] So don't doubt yourself; here are the ten biggest mistakes women make in advancing their careers.

- **Mistake #1:** Not talking about compensation or growth opportunities with your manager at all. By not having the conversation, you will have the most challenging time advancing, even if you do the best work. The people who ask, whether qualified or not, are the ones that advance. Many women do not want to ask for raises or promotions because they feel it's more meaningful if they work hard and their manager notices their value. Or they feel grateful to have the job in the first place. Most often, we don't talk to our managers because we don't have a clear plan or set career goals for ourselves.

- **Mistake #2:** Going into your manager's office with your arms out and asking for more while doing the same role. This is the "what's in it for" me approach. Many companies give raises within a role, and if your company is one of them, then it's ok to assume your 3 percent raise or whatever the going rate is if you're doing a great job. In this case, you are settling for 3 percent and still waiting for someone to notice and advance you.

- **Mistake #3:** Not understanding the worth of your role or how to value your work. Many women don't know the average salary for someone in their position and are paid less on average. When approaching your boss for a raise, align your value with your work, not with what others are making.

Think of the value of your position like a hundred-dollar bill. No matter where the hundred-dollar bill is, or who is in possession of it, it's still worth one hundred dollars. The same is true for *you* and your work; you still hold the same value. Understanding your worth is important at all stages of your career.

- **Mistake #4:** If you are asking more than every nine to twelve months, then you are asking too often—unless there are positions open. Then you should step right up.

- **Mistake #5:** Only checking in once a year on how you are doing. When you wait for a review or a single meeting, you miss opportunities to ensure that you are on the right path. Having regular check-in meetings will ensure that you get to the next position.

- **Mistake #6:** Not being focused on personal growth and development. If you are not teachable, then your manager will not see you as capable of advancing, because what you see is what you get. If you never take time to develop new skills, you will have less chance of being promoted. There is, however, a difference between personal growth and development and racking up degrees and certifications. A degree or certification alone will not get you promoted in most cases.

- **Mistake #7:** Not talking about your accomplishments. Nobody likes the person that runs around the office, showboating every little achievement—because that's annoying. But as women, we are less likely to step up and own our accomplishments, and often we diminish them or see them as insignificant. I can't tell you the number of clients I have worked with that tell me they haven't accomplished anything.

Mainly this happens because women don't see the changes they are making as significant enough to count, or they have humility and see the changes made as a collective effort.

- **Mistake #8:** Not appreciating others who have helped you. Although you do want to give yourself credit, it's important to appreciate and recognize those that have helped you get to this point in your career. Appreciation is key to helping others know that you haven't overlooked their efforts to help you. If you make it all about you, others won't want you to earn a promotion as much.

- **Mistake #9:** Not having your goals in alignment with the company's goals. If you want to add value to the company, then you need to understand what the company's needs are. This will ensure that your efforts are maximized.

- **Mistake #10:** Not presenting your ideas properly or not sharing ideas at all. Many women I talk to tell me that their manager doesn't listen to their ideas, doesn't like their ideas, or puts them in a "parking lot." I've had people tell me that they won't even bring up new ideas at work because no one likes their ideas, and they are never adopted, so they quit sharing ideas. This is a two-fold problem. First, it diminishes the way you feel, and therefore you stopped adding value. You lose because chances are you have other good ideas, but you never share or get credit for them. And the company loses because you are no longer working to make the company better. When we fail to share ideas, we cannot be seen as thought leaders, and vocal thought leaders are often the ones who are selected for promotions.

With a list like that, you might be feeling like advancement is full of landmines.

Earning promotions doesn't have to be difficult. In the upcoming chapters, we will dive deep into the blueprint of your promotion plan and lay out the entire system needed for you to create and present a plan that is chalked full of value. In the next chapter, I'll provide a brief overview of each section so you know that there is a plan that can help you avoid all ten of the biggest career advancement mistakes.

PRAYER

Dear Heavenly Father, You are the One who provides promotion even when the conditions are not perfect. I thank You for my current career and for the many opportunities that You have afforded me. I thank You for giving me a desire to make the world a better place by giving me clear purpose in the work that I do. Lord, You know the desire that I have in my heart to advance my career, grow as leader to help others, and to create an abundant life for my family. I ask, Lord, that You would go before me and make a way if it is Your will and not just mine. Thank You for loving me and allowing me to live a life of peace, fulfillment, and abundance today. I love You, Lord Jesus. Amen.

CHAPTER 16

THE SEVEN-STEP MY PROMOTION PLAN BLUEPRINT

Over the next several chapters, you will learn how to make a My Promotion Plan. Before we dive deep into each section, let's review the sections so that you can start to visualize your promotion plan.

- Step 1: Career Advancement Journey (CAJ). This will be created in the goals chapter. Your CAJ outlines your path for advancement at the company, showing your commitment and desire to grow. The CAJ is optional to include in your plan and, if included, will be the final page.
- Step 2: The Appreciation Letter. Opening with gratitude and appreciation will set the tone that you didn't get here on your own and show that you value your manager.
- Step 3: Accomplishments. It's time to take credit for all of the remarkable accomplishments you have had in the last year or since your latest promotion. Showing your previous

track record is a great way to show your manager that you have been committed and you make a difference already.

- Step 4: Ideas for the future and problems to solve. This is the heart of the promotion plan and will be the largest component of your plan. When you outline your ideas on paper, it allows you to have a fuller expression of the concept and increase the acceptance of the ideas. Solving problems is included in this section because the solutions to the problems are ideas also. This section will allow you to showcase your strategies and be seen as a thought leader, giving you an executive presence.
- Step 5: Personal Development and Growth Plan. To continue to advance and grow professionally, you always want to be learning. The world changes rapidly, and what worked yesterday and today may not work tomorrow. You are always becoming the best version of yourself, and great leaders are learners.
- Step 6: Market value. To understand the value you hold in the market allows you to negotiate your salary with certainty. Knowing how to find your market value can also help you determine which career advancement steps you may want for your future.
- Step 7: Closing. In the closing, you will ask for the promotion you want and open the door to talk about your compensation.

Please don't underestimate this process because of its simplistic nature. It works for those that are willing to invest the time into creating the plan.

For the remainder of the chapter, we will build your promotion plan's foundation and make a schedule for completion.

Before creating your promotion plan, it's important to decide whom you will be presenting your plan to. To ensure the best possible outcome, you likely will want to have more than one person in your promotion meeting.

First, you need to ensure that the people in the meeting have the decision-making power. Whoever controls the promotions and finances needs to be a part of your meeting. This may or may not be your direct manager.

Generally, you will want to invite your direct manager and others who are key decision-makers in the organization.

Only include the people that can make the decisions within the company. For example, do not invite a coworker or a manager that isn't in your division unless you desire to move into their division.

It's always suggested to invite the owner or your manager's manager into the meeting. This will help you to have buy-in higher up in the organization and allow for an additional person to understand your desire to advance.

Once you know who is coming to your meeting, it's time to develop a theme for your plan. The theme will help to tie your entire plan together and set a tone for your overall objective.

Not to over-complicate the concept of a theme, think about the last wedding you attended. Was it country chic, glam, black and white, and so on?

Your promotion plan isn't a wedding. But the reason weddings pick themes is that themes work. Align your plan around a central concept or idea. Most often, if you have a strong company culture, I recommend tying your plan into the culture. It helps to show that your advancement is aligned with the company.

If you don't have a strong company culture, then think about what you are hoping your overall promotion plan will do for the company. It's not uncommon for you to struggle to name your theme before starting your plan. I tell you about it upfront so as you put your promotion plan together, you can develop a theme.

A few themes that I've used are:

- Opportunities for Growth and Change
- Leadership Objectives
- Take Ownership and Expect Others to do the Same

Feel free to use mine or create something that you like more.

In life, we tend to think that people get lucky or have immense amounts of talent, and that's why they can achieve things that others can't. This simply isn't true. Luck is a by-product of setting a goal, having a plan, taking consistent daily actions, and believing that you can achieve an outcome.

Luck Formula

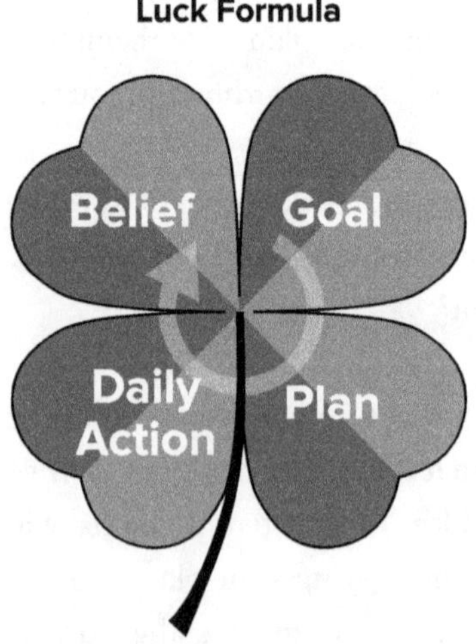

Previously, I shared the power of belief and how I went from not being a runner to running a marathon. I didn't accomplish the marathon solely because I believed. I had to take congruent and consistent actions. When I got home from the first 5K, I thought that was fun, and I'd like to see if I could run a 5K without stopping. I signed up for another 5K and met my goal. A few weeks later, while on vacation at the coast, I woke up and told my husband that I was going to run a marathon.

That morning I ran six miles on the hotel treadmill. I went home and contacted my cousin, Linda, the only person I knew that had run a marathon. She gave me the name of a trainer, and I looked up a training plan. I then looked up the next marathon happening in San Antonio. The race was mid-November, which meant it was possible, but I would have only four months to train.

I laid out my plan, and each day I executed the plan. Over time I found myself enjoying running, and the more miles were getting more manageable. When race day came, I was prepared and completed my first marathon. It had nothing to do with luck and everything to do with a clear desire, decision, planning, preparation, and persistence.

The training part wasn't sexy, and there were times when I didn't know if I was cut out for running. When I started running ten miles, I began to have shooting pains in my feet. That's the day I went to a running store and learned that all running shoes are not created equal.

When I got around the twenty-mile mark, I started having terrible leg cramps. My husband would come and find me lying on the side of the road and stretch me out so I could finish my run for the day.

Most of the runs were good, but there were many challenges along the way: almost getting hit by cars on early morning runs, coming face to face with a deer, chafing, blisters, training in over 104-degree heat. No matter the circumstances, I was determined to run and complete this race. Each day I wasn't focused on the 26.2 miles I would one day need to run to cross the finish line. I was focused on that day's training plan and what it would teach me.

AS YOU BEGIN TO PUT YOUR PROMOTION PLAN TOGETHER, THINK OF THE DAY THAT YOU TURN IN YOUR PLAN AS RACE DAY.

The great thing about the promotion plan process is you don't have to wait for your manager to talk to you about advancement. You get to set the date, and the best time to select the date is now.

I've included a 30-Day No-Fail Promotion Plan Execution Calendar so you will understand the amount of time you can expect to take for each section and what you need to do each day to create your plan. My last plan took me about eighteen hours to complete.

This wasn't my first plan, and I don't want you to put that amount of pressure on yourself, but if you already have a meeting coming up, you will want to fast-track yourself. In general, it takes people about thirty days to develop their plan fully and complete the finishing details.

I suggest that you turn your plan in to your manager on the first Monday of the month and then schedule your meeting to review the plan on a Tuesday. Dr. Robert Cialdini states that people are more open to change at the beginning of a time period. Meaning the first Monday in January is the best day to turn in the plan psychologically.[102]

Companies do most of their hiring at the beginning of the year and have more money in their budgets too. This doesn't mean that you can't or shouldn't turn one in during the fall/ winter months, but instead, you should not drag your feet if it's the prime time.

I didn't have this information when I put my first two plans together. I turned them in in June, and it wasn't the start of the month. I always turned them in on a Monday, but I did it because I didn't want to wait three days to talk about the plan. I was a thinker, and who knows the stories I would have told myself about what my manager thought about the plan if I would have turned it in on a Friday.

Schedule a one-hour meeting to review the plan. It's good to set this up now so that your managers' schedules aren't full. When you schedule the appointment, you can call it a personal development meeting.

When setting up the meeting date and time, consider everyone you would like to have in your meeting. Are they typically in the office on those days? Will you need to invite anyone in virtually? If so, be sure to set up webinar conferencing ahead of time and provide details with the schedule request.

By setting the date of your personal development review, you now have a deadline that you need to take action for. This will help hold you accountable for taking the time each day to do a bit of work. Consistency is key to completing your plan and overcoming procrastination.

Don't put this off.

When we allow ourselves to procrastinate, we actually place more pressure on ourselves to perform well because it has taken us so much time to complete. Therefore, we think that it should be perfect. Most of what we do in life doesn't require perfection. In Dan Sullivan's book, *The 80% Approach*, he teaches to get work to 80 percent. Not expecting yourself to be perfect allows you to get to completion.[103]

A promotion plan that is 80 percent complete is better than a promotion plan that is never completed or one that's completed months later. If you earn a $3,500 raise and take four months longer to turn it in, you never see the $1,166 you could have made during that time. If you earn a $15,000 raise and take four months longer to turn it in, you lose $5,000.

Time is money.

If you find yourself falling into the perfection trap, remind yourself that no one else in the company is even presenting a plan. They are going in and asking for a raise or promotion with empty hands, and often they are getting them. Your plan will stand out because it's different, professional, and adds value back to the company.

If you follow the 30-Day No-Fail Promotion Plan Execution Calendar, you will have an incredible plan, and most days you will only need to spend one hour on your plan. You may have to reprioritize something to find this time.

In life, to get something that we really want, we have to make it a priority. The things that we make priorities get done every day.

Schedule your days now and plan to take one twenty-four-hour period off from all work as a rest day. When we take time to rest and know that we have a day of rest ahead, we can focus more deeply on the work when we are doing it. The important thing is to work the plan on the days that you schedule.

I caution you not to sign up for any other programs or start any other personal development courses during this time. If we allow ourselves to indulge in gaining more information, this is actually a form of busy work and a hidden procrastination tactic. There will be one section of the plan where it's recommended that you use outside resources if needed. This is allowed, but I do caution you not to overthink the process. I've been guilty of this more times than I would like to admit. Busy and unfocused is not productive work; it's busywork. When I start to feel like I'm overthinking things, I think about the Israelites and how their eleven-day trip had them lost in the wilderness for forty years.[104]

Don't get stuck in the wilderness of overthinking or doubt.

Every time you start something and leave it unfinished, you add stress to your life. Everything can wait thirty days. If it's important, then it will still be important six weeks from now.

Set yourself up for success by getting focused each day before you start working on your plan.

TEN FOCUS TOOLS

1. Timing: Most people have the most creativity about one hour after waking. If you are a night owl and do great work at night, then that's fine too. Know yourself and pick the optimal time as not to make it more difficult. Then put it on your schedule—one hour for mindset and time with God and at least one hour for working on your plan.
2. Temperature: If it's too hot or too cold, you will have a hard time focusing, so ensure that the temperature is comfortable.
3. Hydration: Be sure to drink plenty of fresh, filtered water to improve your energy and focus.
4. Grounding: You can walk barefoot outside for twenty minutes or invest in a grounding mat that you can use indoors.
5. Background music: Classical or something soothing like Berry Goldstein. You can use binaural beats to help you get in the alpha state. Listening to the same music for the same task will help your mind engage in the task.
6. Environment: Find a place free of clutter that is comfortable to get work done. Have a good chair and everything you need within arm's reach. Using the same place will train your body that it's time to get to work. I use one couch to meditate on and a different chair and desk for work.
7. Mini break: If you move from one task to another, take two minutes to close your eyes, take deep breaths, and roll your neck and shoulders.
8. Remove distractions: Close tabs on your computer and put your phone across the room. Every time we switch from one task to another, our brains have to readjust, and it takes brainpower you could be using to write your plan.
9. Pray: Each time that you sit down to work on your promotion plan. Pray to God and thank Him for His grace and help. Surrender to God and know that He is there helping you.
10. Stretch, take a walk, or do quick exercises: Getting even a small amount of stretching, walking, or exercise in will improve your energy and creativity. If you get stuck when working, start walking with something to take notes on.

Do what feels right for you. Each person's focus plan will be a bit different. The important thing to know is that focus is only achieved when working on a single item and having our minds consciously in the present moment. Avoid multitasking. We can't focus on two things consciously at the same time. You can try it for yourself. Turn a movie on that you haven't seen before and try playing a game on your phone. You can either play the game or watch the movie; you can't concentrate on both at the same time.

As you continue with your Daily Mind Renewal Routine, focus will become easier for you. If you are not feeling focused, this could be actual resistance. Think about your "why." There will be days that you don't feel like getting up and working on the plan. This is your subconscious mind at work, trying to keep you safe.

YOUR SUBCONSCIOUS MIND IS NOT IN CHARGE OF YOU. GET UP AND GET TO WORK ANYWAY.

To help you save time and improve creativity, complete brain dumps in a journal and then take time to type up your ideas. As you start to type your plan, do not make edits as you build each section. It will take substantially longer because your brain uses different parts for creativity and editing.

At the end of the plan, you will go back and do a completeness check, grammar check, and format your plan. This is done at the end because it's not uncommon for you to continue to think of things for an earlier part of the plan as you build out other sections.

Allow yourself to go back and add additional details, but don't reread your ideas repeatedly. This will cause you to question your plan. I've seen women pour hours into their plan, and it has immense value, but because they have worked on it so closely, they start to create self-doubt.

This is a great time to remember what earning a promotion means for you, the company, and your family.

Each day be consistent in taking the necessary action for that day, and over time, your consistent action will compound. By taking consistent small actions each day, you will build momentum. Be sure to take time for your Daily Mind Renewal Routine. This is how you will continue to strengthen your new programs and confidence.

BUILDING YOUR PLAN

1. Who will I present My Promotion Plan to?
2. What is My Promotion Plan's theme?
3. What date am I setting to turn in My Promotion Plan?
4. At what time each day will I set aside an hour to work on My Promotion Plan?
5. What am I willing to give up to make more time in my schedule?
6. What is my focus plan?
7. What does earning a promotion mean to me?
8. How will my being promoted impact others?

Using the 30-Day No-Fail Promotion Plan Execution Calendar, schedule the days and times that you will work on developing your plan and your rest days.

PRAYER

Dear Heavenly Father, You are Jehovah Jireh, my Provider. Lord, I thank You for caring for me so personally and for going ahead of me to fight my battles. Lord, everything that I have and everything that I am is Yours. Lord, I thank You for my current career, and I ask for Your help in creating a promotion plan that will help me advance my career and Your Kingdom. Lord, I ask that Your will be done, not mine. Lord, I place my hope in You, and I commit to doing my part in faith. I love you, Lord Jesus. Amen.

CHAPTER 17

GOALS TO GUIDE YOUR CAREER ADVANCEMENT JOURNEY

Have you ever woken up and wondered how you got here? In my mid-twenties, I had a lot of those days. As the days, weeks, months, and then years passed, the feeling continued. It's as if after I graduated from college and landed a career, my life went into autopilot with an unknown destination. I was living a mediocre life and spending a lot of time at bars.

Maybe this looks different for you: Netflix binges, social media scrolling, organizing your closet, phone games, or checking emails are just another form of autopilot. This is what life without goals looks like, and over time, it makes us even more complacent and often leaves us feeling unfulfilled.

Change came for me when I started working at the Imagine Wellness Centre, where the owners actually wanted us to set goals, not only for work, but for our personal life too. We would set goals in the following categories: career, finance, health and wellness, relationships, toys and adventures, and spiritual. Not only would we set the goals, but we would share them with each other.

As you set off on your career advancement path, it is essential to set goals and write them down. Writing the goal and then seeing the goals in your own words is powerful. It makes the goal become real in your mind. You now own that goal. Studies show that this process increases our likelihood to accomplish the goal by 42 percent.[105]

In this chapter, we will focus on your career advancement BHAG and your career advancement journey, which is the first piece of your promotion plan. A BHAG is a Big Hairy Audacious Goal. James Collins first coined this term in his book *Good to Great*.[106]

The purpose of a BHAG is to set a goal that you have no idea how you will accomplish. This is more than a stretch goal—it's the ultimate goal.

My personal BHAG was set in November of 2019 to help women obtain one million promotions or raises in ten years.

When I set this goal, I had no clue if the goal could or would be accomplished; it may seem unrealistic for many. After setting this goal, my mind has gone to work subconsciously figuring out how to accomplish it. At the time, I had just launched my online course. But my marketing wasn't fully optimized. That goal and the challenges to getting the word out led me to write this book, develop a keynote speech, and create the Inner Circle Mastermind, a course in which leaders can help their teams develop promotion plans in their organizations. I ended up creating a multiplier effect that I hadn't even thought of when I first set the goal.

As you set your career advancement BHAG, you want to avoid four traps that hold people back.

First, don't let other people already having a position limit you from thinking that you can't have that position. It's true that at this moment, another person may be in that role. But that shouldn't change your desire for achievement or stop you from taking steps toward that position. I once told my manager who was the COO that I wanted to be the next COO. That could have been perceived as a threat. But I wasn't telling her that I wanted to kick her out. In my mind, my taking on that role was at least ten years out. What I was doing was planting a seed. Every leader needs a successor, and when you enlist others in your goals, they can help you obtain what you want. Sharing with others that you want to be in the role one day gives you an advantage. When people know what you desire, they can help you achieve it.

Second, don't limit yourself by your current skillset or the career advancement paths that a company has. Maybe you are on one track now, and your track doesn't lead to the position that you truly desire. There is always a way to make new paths, and you can learn new skills to advance into the roles. This is part of the subconscious work that your mind will do to help you achieve your goal.

Third, don't limit yourself to positions that already exist within your company. Over time, companies create new positions, and your desired position can be created. The world is always changing, and positions will come and go based on those changes. As companies grow, the need for new positions also arises.

The fourth trap that holds people back is thinking they can't hold a position because they are not like the current person in the role. You may not possess the same qualities and skills as the person in the role currently. Yes, you may need some of their skills to be successful, but you don't have to be like this person. This is especially important for women.

Now it's time for you to set your career BHAG. Write it down, and don't worry about how you will achieve it.

REMEMBER, WITH GOD,
ANYTHING IS POSSIBLE.

Anything. Don't overthink this; you don't have to know every detail in how you will accomplish the goal.

Once you have your BHAG, let's take a look at the positions you might obtain on the road to that position, and map out a career advancement journey. Having a Career Advancement Journey (CAJ) was not a part of my original design. It came about through a suggestion by my manager after creating promotion plans became the standard for advancing in the company.

As a manager to others, it's helpful to understand my team members' desires and ambitions. As I manage from day to day, I use this tool to help determine who to bring into new projects.

It's important to remember that a CAJ is not an ultimatum for your manager, yourself, or God. It's a simple plan to understand your career advancement desires. Things will likely evolve. You may choose to change the direction of your advancement.

By having a CAJ, your manager will be aware of your desire to grow, and you will also learn if your path is in alignment with the company's vision.

The career advancement acceleration journey consists of three parts.

- Part 1: Position title. I.e., CEO, VP of Sales, Director, Supervisor, etc.
- Part 2: Training. As we discussed earlier, self-awareness is key to career advancement. List the hard and soft skills you need to develop within this role. By identifying your areas of opportunity, it will invite others to help train you in those areas and allow you to get the training you need.
- Part 3: Know the role. List out the main responsibilities of the role you desire. Suppose you are listing a position that does not yet exist within the company. In that case, write out what the company will accomplish by having this role. This can help your manager understand what the role will be responsible for and plant a seed of possibility in the manager's mind.

Once you've gone through this process, post your CAJ in your office or keep it in an easily accessible area to reference throughout the year.

As you begin to map out your CAJ, ensure that you don't skip any rungs on the ladder. If you are unrealistic in your career advancement journey, you will put yourself at risk for having a lack of awareness around advancement.

For example, if you are an executive assistant for the Chief Marketing Officer, your next career step will not be the Vice President of Marketing. To make the advancement more successful, create micro-steps in which you can be successful.

In this example, micro-steps could include Assistant to Marketing Director, Marketing Director, Senior Marketing Director, and Vice President of Marketing.

Micro-steps allow room for more promotions year after year.

When I was promoted from the Service Operation Manager position to the Vice President of Operations rather than the Chief Operating Officer position, this gave me the chance to grow and develop my skills within that role, skills that helped me advance the following year to the Chief Operating Officer. It also allowed me to earn another promotion and salary increase.

Each business has a different structure for advancement. If you are unsure how promotion typically works in your organization, speak with the human resource department to obtain career advancement paths. The path can be used as a guide to help you know the current steps for advancement. On occasion, you will find that the path you are on does not lead to your BHAG career goal. If this happens, you have a couple of options to consider, including making a lateral change that will put you on the path you are looking to go in. If you can't make a lateral change, then come up with a training plan to obtain the position's knowledge without actually holding the position. If your company is smaller and doesn't have a human resource department, then don't concern yourself with how this typically works, and continue to create your plan.

BUILDING YOUR PLAN, DAYS ONE AND TWO (TWO HOURS): CREATE YOUR CAJ

In your journal, take the time consider the next five career positions you would like. Then list the areas you need training in to obtain these positions. Finally, list the basic responsibilities that these positions entail.

Here's an outline for you to work with:

My Career Advancement BHAG:

Take action now by completing your **Career Advancement Journey**:

- Position:
  - Training:
  - Responsibilities:
- Position:
  - Training:
  - Responsibilities:

- Position:
    - Training:
    - Responsibilities:
- Position:
    - Training:
    - Responsibilities:
- Position:
    - Training:
    - Responsibilities:

PRAYER

Dear Heavenly Father, as I start to plan my career advancement journey, I ask that You give me wisdom and understanding on the direction that You want me to go. I thank You for allowing me the opportunity to serve as a leader at work and at home. Lord, I ask that You help me to be brave and bold as I seek to reach my fullest potential in my career and life. Jesus, I freely give You all of me to complete Your good and perfect will. Lord, give me peace. I surrender to You, Lord, and ask that You use me as a vessel to do Your good and perfect work. I haven't always believed in myself and my ability to advance, but with Your grace, strength, and provision, I know that anything is possible. Let Your grace be my strength and Your wisdom be present in my CAJ. I love You, Lord Jesus, and ask these things in Your Holy Name. Amen.

CHAPTER 18

APPRECIATION LETTER

Writing appreciation letters is something I highly recommend.

This became a part of my own planning after being promoted to the Vice President of Operations because I was so grateful to the other executives who helped support my growth further. I had the opportunity to attend a live event with the founder. I hadn't been to a large conference in a while, and it reminded me how valuable in-person events were for my personal development.

There are always pearls that I can pull out and bring back to make the company better. Attending this event gave me ideas that were valuable to my second promotion plan. Furthermore, it helped spark creativity by opening my mind to a new experience.

When I went to make my plan, I wrote a letter of gratitude and appreciation for the opportunities I had been given.

Your appreciation letter should be no more than one page long and could be as little as a couple of paragraphs. The idea of the letter is to recognize that you wouldn't be in the position that you are today or have the opportunities that you have if it wasn't for the support of others.

This letter is rare for most managers, as their employees will rarely show appreciation for them, much less write a letter. The truth is that your manager has helped you to get where you are today.

Write the letter from your heart with gratitude for all that they have done. Then give specific examples of the activities that you appreciated and that grew you the most. You can recognize other managers and team members if desired.

Do not include things that you did not enjoy or don't desire to do again. When you write your appreciation items, this will indirectly tell your manager what you like and want more of in the future.

I once had a client ask me what they should say in their letter when they felt that their manager didn't do anything to help. When your manager isn't directly helping you grow and achieve things, they are still helping you. Always look for the silver lining.

In this case, I suggest that she tell her manager that she appreciates the autonomy and space that her manager gives her to make decisions within the role. Take time to think about how your manager's actions or inactions lead to your growth.

Appreciating their management/leadership style is an easy thing to do. More importantly, it's an hones t letter. You most certainly do not want to make up a false letter to flatter someone. Not only will you know that it's false, but your manager will know that it's false too.

STAY POSITIVE AND HONEST AND INCLUDE WHATEVER FEELS RIGHT IN YOUR HEART, AND YOU WILL DO GREAT.

At the time of creating the letter, I didn't realize that giving credit and including your manager as part of the reason you were successful is actually a negotiating technique. By "accusing" your manager of being helpful and instrumental in your growth, they feel responsible for a part of your success today and in the future.

The appreciation letter is not the time to ask for a promotion, talk compensation, or talk about your accomplishments. You will get to do all of these things later on in the plan. The letter is meant to show genuine gratitude and appreciation for your managers.

If possible, include everyone attending your meeting in the letter. If you don't work directly with the owner and feel that your manager does an outstanding job, you could compliment them on choosing incredible leadership or providing a vision that drives you to want to do more.

Here is an example of an appreciation letter for a manager that has helped you:

Dear Sue,

I wanted to take a moment to thank you for your support over the past year. Having the opportunity to work at Salt and Light has given me many opportunities, some of which I did not expect. Thank you for allowing me to try new things and for bringing me into some large company projects.

You've taught me so much about budgets, customer service, and taking care of team members. These experiences have been invaluable, and I am grateful for the opportunities you have given me to continue growing and learning.

Working at Salt and Light is more than a job. It's become a way of life. Your leadership style and lessons have molded me into a better leader, and for that, I am eternally grateful.

Having the opportunity to attend the John Maxwell conference has proved invaluable, as it continues to spark innovation and ideas that can further enhance Salt and Light.

I look forward to the upcoming year as we continue to grow Salt and Light. Thank you for being a blessing in my life.

Sincerely,

Mary Guirovich

Here is an example of an appreciation letter for a manager that hasn't helped you:

Dear Sue,

I wanted to take a moment to thank you for the ability to have autonomy in my position. Working at Salt and Light has given me many opportunities, some of which I did not expect. Thank you for allowing me to try new things and for trusting me to implement new ideas.

Your hands-off approach has helped me grow exponentially, as it challenged me to find solutions and make things happen. I've never had so much freedom, and I genuinely appreciate being able to make an impact in my department.

Working at Salt and Light is more than a job. It's become a way of life. Your leadership style has molded me into a better leader. Because of your approach, I take more responsibility, risks, and make high-level decisions, all of which have helped me grow as a person.

Thank you for allowing me to attend the John Maxwell conference. It has proved invaluable as it continues to spark innovation and ideas that can further enhance Salt and Light.

I look forward to the upcoming year as we continue to grow Salt and Light together.

Sincerely,

Mary Guirovich

You can see that in both examples, the focus is on appreciation and that the letters are 100 percent positive. It's like your mom said, growing up: if you can't say anything nice, then don't say anything at all.

Now it's your turn to create an appreciation letter for your promotion plan.

BUILDING YOUR PLAN, DAYS THREE AND FOUR (TWO HOURS): WRITE YOUR APPRECIATION LETTER

1. Write a one-page appreciation letter to whomever you will be presenting the plan.
2. Type your letter up and make revisions as needed

PRAYER

Dear Heavenly Father, I thank You for my managers and the guidance that they give me. Lord, I ask that You help me write a letter that will show my sincere gratitude and love for them. In your Holy Name, I pray. Amen.

CHAPTER 19

OWNING YOUR ACCOMPLISHMENTS

Speaking to your accomplishments without all the showboating is an art. There aren't many people who enjoy someone running around the office like they are the king of the world and taking credit for everything that is happening. People who act this way can only feel successful if they are continually validated because they harbor deep insecurities.

As a manager and future executive, you have to know how to handle talking about your accomplishments with class to get the credit you deserve. This is exactly what the accomplishment section of your promotion plan will do for you.

The truth is most women work hard and wait to be noticed. The problem is our managers are busy doing their work, and unless you are running around telling everyone what you've done, they might not notice. And if they do notice, they may not have equated the true value of the accomplishment.

The accomplishment section was added to the promotion plan

blueprint for my second plan. I added it in because I felt the need to update my leaders on the previous objectives. It was exciting to scroll back through my first plan and see all of the items that had been implemented. Radical changes had occurred in one year. Once I listed the updates, I listed other accomplishments that I had achieved over the past year. This allows you to show progress and the ability to succeed in your current role.

Often clients will tell me that they don't have many accomplishments. I find that hard to believe. Most people, especially women, do not actively seek to get a promotion if they haven't been doing their job well and aren't positively impacting the company. I've realized that many women don't see the value in what they have accomplished and second guess if they should include it.

List all of your accomplishments, even the ones that might seem small. Don't underestimate your accomplishments and contribution to your company. As you list your accomplishments, think not only about the task or projects you've done, but the quantitative outcomes.

If you honestly can't think of many accomplishments, then you have a few options.

- Option one: Start to make improvements in your workplace now, so you have accomplishments.
- Option two: List your top three accomplishments so that the list will not look like it's your only accomplishments.
- Option three: Leave this section out for your first promotion plan. Your past value isn't the only factor in advancing your career.

List only the accomplishments since your last promotion unless you are going for an executive role. For an executive role, you will want to pull your top accomplishments from across your career with the company to make an accomplishment section that aligns with your desired position.

This section may not be the most comfortable for some of you to write. Don't allow these emotions to overwhelm your subconscious.

WOMEN ARE KNOWN TO HAVE MORE HUMILITY AND SEE ACCOMPLISHMENTS AS A COLLECTIVE. SO IT'S NATURAL FOR YOU TO HAVE UNEASY FEELINGS. BUT DON'T ALLOW THEM TO CONTROL YOU—LEAD WITH STRONG, POSITIVE EMOTIONS.

When putting together your accomplishments, you will want to group them by categories to make them easier to digest.

To get started, pull out a journal and begin a brain dump of all of the accomplishments you can think of. Don't worry about the order, and don't judge the value; simply list them.

If you find the brain dump challenging, then use the following list of categories to help you get started.

Please note that you likely will not have accomplishments in all of the categories, and it's not uncommon for you to create a category that's not listed.

Example categories:

TEAM	Team Member Development Hiring Helping Others Advance Training Others Other's Accomplishments if you helped manage/lead them New Roles Developed Team Members Removed/Replaced
SYSTEMS	Systems Created Systems Improved Systems Removed
MARKETING	Marketing Developed Marketing Results/Stats Marketing Sources Marketing Events
REVENUE	Revenue Increases Revenue Streams Revenue Processes Investments
INTERNAL OPERATIONS	Onboarding Reviews Recognition/Appreciation Team Building HR MGMT HR-Related Matters
INTERNAL EVENTS	Creation Improvements Enhancement Systems Flow Processes Revenue

IT	Management Systems Enhancements Software Expenditures Ticket Times Program Development Hardware Upgrades Security Efficiency
SERVICE	Customer Service Surveys/Net Promoter Scores Systems Collections Attrition Enhancements Client Satisfaction Processes Client Results
CULTURE/OFFICE	Creation Systems Development Celebrations Management Enhancements Retention
INTERNAL	Organizing Cleaning Building Upgrades Enhancements Decor New Equipment
KEY PERFORMANCE INDICATORS (KPIS)	Significant Increases Significant Decreases New KPIs Implemented

CHARITY WORK	Positions Held Ideas Implemented Improvements Systems Volunteer work
PERSONAL DEVELOPMENT	Certifications Courses Completed Advancement Levels Skills Obtained Skills Refined

BUILDING YOUR PLAN, DAYS FIVE TO SEVEN (THREE HOURS): OWNING YOUR ACCOMPLISHMENTS

1. Brainstorm your accomplishments in a journal.
2. Quantify the results when applicable.
3. Type of your accomplishments by category.

PRAYER

Abba, my Heavenly Father, I thank You for the accomplishments that You have helped me with at work. I know that my successes come from You. I thank You for the many gifts that You have given me that allow me to do the work that You have prepared for me in advance to do. Lord, I ask that You enable me to remember my achievements with ease and not to doubt their value. Thank You for Your help, Lord Jesus. In Your Holy Name, I pray. Amen

CHAPTER 20

ADDING VALUE THROUGH NEW IDEAS

The fastest way to become more valuable to your company today is to develop strategies and to be seen as a thought leader. Managers become executives because they know how to lead with vision and develop successful strategies.

This section will be the heart of your plan. When I put my first promotion plan together, I led with strategy. I knew that I had ideas that would have a profound impact on the company. I was capable of seeing what the company needed to do to make changes and correct persistent problems.

Yet, every time I spoke with my manager, it seemed difficult to share my vision and gain traction. When I struggled to gain traction, I doubted my ideas. It made me question if I had the right strategies in mind. This challenged me to dig deeper, which only reinforced my belief in the ideas themselves. The problem wasn't the strategies; it was my inability to communicate and present them in a compelling and meaningful way.

Typically, the higher up you are in an organization, and the more you are paid in an organization, the more your input is valued. It's a subconscious pattern that even the best leaders fall victim to. They judge the idea based on the person that provides it more than the idea itself.

There are many reasons for not adopting new ideas. Most organizations do not have a system for bringing ideas to the table, and managers are left overrun with suggestions that they never move forward. Sometimes your manager may feel threatened that you had a good idea before they did. Most often, managers assume that they will be responsible for implementing the new idea and don't have the time.

Whatever the reason, when a manager turns down too many ideas, employees will quit sharing them. Managers are generally vastly unaware that this is happening. When that happens, employees see themselves as less valuable, leaving many feeling stuck in their career, even when performing well in their roles. That is why this section is such an important part of your plan, because it showcases your future value, allows your manager to understand the impact you want to make, helps your manager see your ideas more clearly, and allows you to be seen as a thought leader.

When you were hired, you may have been given a job description, a checklist, or were trained on key tasks. Doing your tasks makes you a good employee. Becoming an advancing leader means seeing more and doing more to advance the company. Having a strategy that advances the company is the key to your advancement.

SUCCESSFUL STRATEGY NEARLY ALWAYS INVOLVES CHANGE. YOU MUST BE OPEN TO CHANGING THE WAY THINGS ARE DONE. WITHOUT CHANGE, ADVANCEMENTS CAN'T BE MADE.

You don't want to embrace change for the sake of change. But you do want to fall in love with the idea of change.

If you look at the history of America, you can see how change has impacted the world. A new invention is a simple form of change. When the TV came to market, it changed the way people received the news, the speed at which they received information, and it opened up a new means of advertising. Today it shapes our culture.

Change can also come in the form of improving a process. An improved process can lower cost, increase efficiency, and create consistent outcomes. Henry Ford creating the assembly line for the Model T car is an example of an improved process. By refining the process, creating a Model T car went from over twelve hours down to one hour and thirty-three minutes. When you can make a car in less than a tenth of the original time, your labor costs also decrease substantially.[107] A strategy like this would help you earn a promotion.

Embracing change ensures that your company won't become outdated and eventually obsolete. New processes, products, or technology are always on the horizon. Trying to fight this fact is about as useless as trying to tell the sun not to come up tomorrow. When companies fail to embrace the changes in technology, they lose out on what could be.

In 1975, Steve Sasson worked for Kodak. He built and patented the first digital camera. When he took the idea to his manager, it was turned down. He was told that no one would want to look at pictures on a TV screen.[108] The marketing department didn't want anything to do with the camera because the digital camera would cannibalize their film sales. In 2012, Kodak filed for bankruptcy. Although the company is still around today, the majority of their business has shifted into new markets.

When thinking about your strategy, the outcome of the idea is more important than the idea itself. A simple strategy could include asking for an upsell at the cash register with every purchase. Have you ever noticed how they ask you to purchase their special of the day at the gas station? This is not a fluke. When asked, they have found that customers will buy more than if they are not asked. At the same time, there is no additional cost to the store for having the employee ask, and there isn't a negative effect on the customer. Most consumers will not be turned off by a smiling employee, offering them a special candy bar.

The impact of this idea could be huge. Consider that the store gets one thousand visitors per day, and 10 percent of customers purchase an additional product for one dollar. That would equate to one hundred dollars in additional sales per day and an additional $36,500 in sales per year in a single store. Now multiply this effect over 250 stores across the country. This idea of offering a single one-dollar product at checkout would be a 9.1-million-dollar idea.

To take it a step further, you could work to improve the results. Through experimentation, you learn that asking the customer while holding the product in your hand and smiling with eye contact increases the conversion rate by an additional 10 percent. Now the idea is worth $73,000 per store and is an 18.25-million-dollar idea.

Over time, it is a simple strategy that produces tremendous results.

When you develop a strategy, think about the outcomes that will be achieved. It doesn't have to be glamorous to generate four key benchmarks: cash, growth, customer satisfaction, and overall return on investment (ROI).

FOUR KEY STRATEGIC AREAS FOR SUCCESS

CASH

Cash is essential to an organization because it determines its ability to run its operations, provides investment opportunities, and fuels growth opportunities. Cash on hand is the amount of money that a business has in hand, in the bank, and most often accessible within ninety days. This is the money that is used to pay rent, payroll, and other expenses. This money gets replenished by cash generated from core business operations. Understanding your company's cash flow will help you understand your company's ability to invest in research and development opportunities that can help fuel growth.

Think of ways to increase revenue with your current product offerings, accelerate your customers' payments, reduce expenses, delay payments, decrease labor costs, etc.

GROWTH

Growth is essential to the longevity of your company. It includes your company's ability to bring new products and services to the marketplace—the ability to enter new markets to widen your potential customer base and could include mergers and acquisitions. A new market could be a new customer segment or movement into another country or region. Success in the growth category is most dependent on the market's demand and alignment with your product and services. One of the easiest ways to grow is to offer a new product or service to your existing customers. Consider offerings that your company could add on to or new offerings that would serve your current customers' needs.

In your promotion plan, you may present a specific idea to your company to add on, or you may give the idea of considering adding on a new product or service based on your research and understanding what clients are more likely to buy. Part of the solution would be to survey current clients on their needs to determine the offerings and possibly add an upsell to an existing offering.

You may also discuss the need for innovation in your plan. Many companies, especially smaller ones, do not have a plan for research and development. Understanding how to stay relevant in your industry is paramount to your company's continued success.

CUSTOMER SATISFACTION

Customer happiness is the number-one indicator of a company's future success. When your customers are happy, they will purchase more, refer more, connect you with their community, and will want to pay their satisfaction forward. Customers pay their satisfaction forward by giving reviews, testimonials, referrals, and by becoming a volunteer ambassador. In today's social media hype, volunteer ambassadors can easily refer your company to not only their inner circle but their much larger group of friends via online groups and open forums. It's not enough to have satisfied customers. You need to have raving fans. Gone are the days where people need you to educate them about your products or services. What hasn't changed is the human desire to feel loved, appreciated, and special. Companies with excellent customer service treat their employees well, train them properly, and empower them to go beyond what's expected. To be great, you must do the unexpected and think of the customers' needs before it exists.

RETURN

Return or ROI is your company's financial gain in business or investments. The key is to continue to grow the return while minimizing the risk. Investments include but are not limited to financial investments. They can also include higher sales, increased revenues, bigger profits, reduced overhead or production costs, higher employee retention, or increased brand preference. Simple ways to improve your return are to decrease expenses. Evaluate where the company is spending money and what other opportunities there are to reduce those costs. Review contracts that are coming to an end to negotiate lower rates or switch to a newer service that may be a superior product. The market and pricing are always changing, so check in with the companies you are doing business with. They may be now offering their services at a lower rate in which you can have your payment adjusted. Another way to increase your return is to raise your prices. When your products, service, and quality are good, people will pay a premium price even when they could get a similar product at lower prices. Returns can also be seen through investing in your team's training, employee benefits, customer appreciation events, and even online marketing. When your team is trained and equipped with the resources they need to do their job with ease, they are more efficient, and they get more enjoyment out of their work. In addition, they may make fewer mistakes when you invest in employee benefits or additional vacation time, and your ability to hire and train better personnel will likely increase. When holding a customer appreciation event, you may not make money on the event, but you will increase customers' retention rate. When marketing, you not only get direct sales, but you get brand recognition and increased traffic to your website. Although these returns are harder to track, you will see them through retention rates and referrals, both for new customers and new hires.

IDEAS, PROBLEMS, AND SOLUTIONS

To get started in building this strategy section of your promotion plan, you will begin with a brain dump in your journal. Write down as many ideas as you can think of to improve your company, and write down the problems you see your company is currently experiencing.

> IT'S CRITICAL NOT TO JUDGE YOUR IDEAS AT THIS POINT. THERE ISN'T ANYTHING THAT YOU CAN WRITE DOWN THAT IS WRONG OR FOOLISH. EVERYTHING IS WELCOMED IN YOUR BRAIN DUMP.

Write in bullet points or phrases to not get locked in on one idea or problem. People are often said to have crazy ideas until they come to fruition; then they're geniuses.

Once you do a brain dump, you can then organize your ideas, which will make them easier to digest. Once you have your ideas organized into categories, you will start to flush out each one to solve a particular problem.

Each item will have three parts.

1. A simple statement of the idea.
2. A statement(s) of why the idea is needed.
3. An explanation of the solution(s) the idea offers.

Part one and part three are pretty straightforward, as you will see in the basic example below. In the second part, we want to take all emotions out of the statements and stick with the reasons why the idea is needed.

Here's an example:

- **Idea**: Repaint the front door
- **Why it's needed** (bad example with emotion):
    - Our current door is an awful yellow color, and I don't like the color yellow.
    - Every day when I walk into the office, I am angry because the door has black marks all over it, and I have to spend twenty minutes of my time cleaning it.
    - My coworkers are sloppy and get grease on the door.
- **Why it's needed** (good example without emotion):
    - Our door's light color isn't the best reflection of the clean appearance our company stands for.
    - Each day, it takes twenty minutes to clean the door; over a year, that's nearly eighty-seven hours.
    - Grease stains appear throughout the day.

By including why it's needed and providing this level of detail without emotion, your manager will now fully understand why you want to make the change and what some of the benefits will be to the company. Then you want to show that you have real solutions. For this example, here is a straightforward way to address what's needed:

- Repaint the door a different color to reduce the appearance of stains.
- Use a paint that is more naturally stain resistant.
- Remind employees not to touch the front of the door.
- Enlist the janitorial service to wipe down the door as needed.

By providing a list of solutions, you show that you have thought beyond the problem to actionable solutions. You also show that you want to raise your company's perception and profile, which is something that may have never occurred to your manager. Maybe they park in the back and never see the front door. Your awareness and strategy raise their awareness.

If the idea warrants it, include visuals or projected results for quantitative activities.

When building out this section, it's recommended to present a minimum of fifteen to thirty ideas or problems. Your manager isn't going to see the value or like everything that you bring to the table. By having a robust list, you will give yourself more opportunities for approval, implementation, and eventually earning you future promotions.

So what ideas and problems should you solve? You should give the most input in the direction that you are trying to take your career. Depending on your field and size of business, this is different for every person. You don't want to list problems or ideas that you have already been asked to implement or things that are part of your everyday job that you have been failing to perform.

Also include your ideas for other departments. This will show that you understand how the organization is working together and that you're invested in helping the whole team win. You won't likely be the one to implement those ideas, but you will open doors to start to learn about other departments.

Remember, this section of your promotion plan starts with knowledge and creativity. Give yourself enough space, time, and rest to bring the right energy to this exercise. Meditation, visualization, and prayer will help reduce stress and allow you to be more creative. Ask God to help you develop the ideas that will best serve your team, customers, and business. Pray and think about these things before going to bed.

GOD TALKS TO US IN OUR DREAMS AND CAN HELP GIVE US THE IDEAS THAT WE NEED. GOD WILL BE TALKING TO YOU, BUT YOU HAVE TO LISTEN AND NOT JUDGE HIS IDEAS.

Stay alert and pay attention to the world around you, and you will uncover more ideas and solutions than you ever thought possible.

Finally, you may need more information. This is the time when you may need to consult with others, read a book, or conduct online research to help you develop ideas and solve problems. Remember that you don't have to have the perfect solution to all of your ideas. Providing a few solutions will be enough to get you through turning in the plan and getting your manager on board to think about solutions.

Select resources that will be meaningful to your office. If meetings in your office are a problem, you can read a book on having better meetings and then adopt those solutions.

Continue to do your Daily Mind Renewal Routine, as this will help you to stay creative.

Remember, your ideas are good. We all tend to be our own worst critics.

Once you complete this section, ask yourself, "Are these the best ideas and strategies that I have today?" If the answer is yes, then you have done your job.

As you build out this section, remember to keep everything organized by category to make the information easily digestible. As you read through your ideas and solve the problems, you will likely start to think of other accomplishments you have had. This is normal, and you can go and add them to your accomplishment list.

BUILDING YOUR PLAN, DAYS EIGHT TO THIRTEEN (TWELVE HOURS): ADDING VALUE THROUGH NEW IDEAS

1. Make a list of any challenges in your company.
2. Make a list of any new ideas that you have.
3. Type up your challenges/ideas by category.
4. For each challenge/idea, list the idea, why it's needed in bullet points in a non-emotional way, and include your solutions for each item.
5. If needed, seek outside resources, books, mentors, and courses to help you develop this section.

PRAYER

Dear Heavenly Father, I thank You for allowing me to identify current challenges within my company and for providing me with ideas that will make a significant impact in the lives of our customers and team. Lord, I ask that You help me be confident in my ideas and that the solutions come quickly. I surrender to You, Lord, and ask You to guide the pen with which I write. I love You, Lord Jesus, and I'm grateful for Your help and never-ending love. In Your Holy Name, I pray. Amen.

CHAPTER 21

PERSONAL DEVELOPMENT

All through our lives, we're told that one day we'll finish school. We've confused that message with the idea that one day we'll have learned enough. But I've found that the end of formal education is just that: the end of formal education. Most companies won't require you to invest in personal development, but top leaders are always learning.

The truth is, no matter what type of formal education you have, it will not provide all of the knowledge that you need to continue to grow and advance in your career. The world changes so rapidly that often things we learned two years ago are no longer relevant today, or new information is discovered that changes everything.

Imagine you're a marketing major and have a career in marketing for a small company. You went to school in the early to mid-2000s. They didn't teach you about social media advertising because Facebook, Instagram, YouTube, etc., might not have been in existence. Today your business will be at a disadvantage in social media marketing because no one knows how to do it. You'll have a hard time learning on the job because no one can teach you. You could choose to ignore social media marketing, but that will only work for a while. And if you switch jobs, you will lack a major skill in the world of marketing today. As the world continues to advance and advertisements change, you have to change too. You have to know how the different platforms work, how to optimize the results of each platform, and who is on different platforms.

All of this goes to show how important it is to not solely rely on our formal education. Personal development and growth will continue to give you an edge as you advance your career. It will help you to remain relevant, build your skillset, and expand the way you think. All great executives dedicate time to personal development.

For your promotion plan, you will create a one-page personal development and growth plan. You will want to pull out your CAJ as you start to craft your personal development and growth plan. Think about the skills you need to obtain to get to the next level in your career and to knock your current position out of the park.

It's best to pick two to four major skills you want to work on over the year. It could be something specific like learning Quickbooks, or it could be a broader topic like improving leadership or presenting skills. By picking only two to four skills to work on, you will be able to dive deeper into the subject and have better mastery.

WHEN YOU DIG FOR OIL, YOU DON'T FIND IT ONE INCH DEEP AND ONE MILE ACROSS; YOU FIND OIL BY DIGGING A MILE DOWN.

The same is true for our learning. Sometimes less is more, so we can learn on a deeper level and retain more valuable information. For even better results, break your year into sections and devote a quarter or six months to deeply developing a skill that will make you an obvious choice in your next role.

Once you have written down the major areas you want to grow and develop, then confirm how these areas will bring you closer to your career advancement goals. You confirm the personal development idea by identifying how it aligns to improving a skill you need to improve in your current position or into your next position. Once you have confirmed alignment, start to flesh out the areas of development by researching learning opportunities.

Learning opportunities could include online courses, seminars, workshops, masterminds, mentors/coaches, books, travel, certifications, local classes, etc.

Online courses are great because they have multiple learning opportunities from watching videos, completing worksheets, and sometimes including a mentoring component. Online courses allow you to see things in action.

Seminars and workshops are great opportunities because you learn from the pros, have time dedicated to travel to the event, and they allow you to network with others. A seminar is typically more of a speaker format where you will learn and are motivated. Workshops are more hands-on and allow you to leave with work done or, at a minimum, started.

Mastermind groups provide opportunities to connect with others who are in a similar business. Masterminding is collaborative and allows you to learn from other people's strengths, and it also allows you to share yours. Mastermind groups are a great way to forge connections and build relationships that can serve you and your company throughout your lifetime. The best mastermind groups have a monetary investment associated with them.

Coaches and mentors are people whom you look up to and desire to learn from. A mentor takes a special interest in your life and helps to guide you toward your desired goals. They also help you work through difficult situations and conversations. Your mentors could be within your company or outside of your company. Many people are open to mentoring you, but you need to start the conversation and ask. Mentors can be older or younger than you. Age alone is not what gives a person wisdom and knowledge. You may already have mentors in your organization. When selecting a mentor, be intentional, and communicate clearly why you want the other person to mentor you. When they can see specifically what is needed, they are more likely to want to mentor you. Mentorship could be free or paid, depending on the person. A paid mentor could even be called a coach, although coaching, when appropriately done, is different from mentoring. A mentor uses their wisdom from experience to teach and help guide you. A coach may or may not have been in your specific situation and helps you, among other things, think of answers already present inside you. Coaches and mentors are invaluable as you can fast-track your success by learning from their knowledge and experiences. As a bonus, you can access their networks and have the support and courage you need to take the next step.

Books are one of the most powerful tools that many people never take advantage of. Other than free mentoring, books are the most economical way to learn powerful and applicable information. You can gain wisdom from past generations and in-depth knowledge from current experts.

When selecting your books, talk to others in the field that you are interested in studying. Or reach out to five to ten people you respect and ask for their top-ten book list. Look at the list and look for overlap. Start with those books.

It's best to study the books and experience them. You do this by being active with the book. Take notes, underline or highlight items, and act on what the author recommends you to do. A book can motivate you when you read it, or it can change your life when you experience and put it into practice.

When I was a new mom, audiobooks became my best friend. To this day, I still love them. To study the audiobook, I bookmark items and take notes. If the book is powerful, I purchase a physical copy to re-read and implement the bits I otherwise would have missed.

Traveling is another great way to learn because you have different experiences. Life in and of itself can constantly show you ways to improve your company. When you experience staying in a hotel, flying on a plane, or traveling to a new location, you have an opportunity to learn about other people and how they do things. This is especially important if you want to help your company expand into a country or region you are not familiar with. How do people talk there? What do they value? What special customs do they have? Many people will not include travel on their personal growth and development plan but can still benefit through work or family travel.

Taking a course and earning a certificate are additional ways to learn. As we discussed, certification for the sake of certification, unless required by your employer, is not necessary to earn a promotion or raise. Always remember the power is not in having a certification and completing a course. Earning the certificate is usually the easy part. Think about how you will implement what you learn. Be sure to communicate and think about the impact that the certification will have on you and the company. When I worked in restaurants, I was certified to teach the ServeSafe Food and ServeSafe Alcohol classes. This benefited the company because it cut down on time and cost for new employees to become trained and ready to work.

Local classes are often offered in your community for a variety of topics. Years ago, when Instagram was new, I attended a local church class with my manager to learn how to set up a profile and get started with Instagram. There are many free or low-cost resources available to you. Stop by the library, ask your network, and look at the events section on social media.

There are many other ways to learn, and you can include them in your plan or add them to your training. It's common to create a combination of learning activities that will help you to grow and develop in your career. This section doesn't have to be a perfect connect-the-dot, but rather the launchpad to get the support and resources you need to learn, develop, and grow.

While researching your personal development opportunities, identify the financial investment. You don't have to list the resources' investments on the personal development guide, but it is helpful for you to know what the investments are. I use the word investment over cost, or expense, intentionally because money spent on learning specific skills that will help you advance are investments into yourself and the company.

Smart companies know that it pays to invest in their team's advancement. When companies fail to invest in their employees, they can lose money through unrecognized revenue.

A common question is, "Can I include personal development goals that don't relate specifically to the company?" Yes, you can. I suggest that the majority of your plan relates specifically to the company and that you have a reason for listing the other items.

For example, I once put that I wanted to write a book in my development plan. I put this in my plan for two specific reasons. First, my manager had written books before, so I knew that he was familiar with the process. I was looking to get insight and help from him. Second, the book I originally wanted to write was on systems, and I believed that we could use this as a marketing tool for our business.

No matter what you put in your plan, you have to ask yourself what I call the *Big Question.*

ARE YOU WILLING TO PAY FOR THE TRAINING IF YOUR COMPANY DOESN'T COVER THE INVESTMENT?

If you didn't answer yes to this question, I would reconsider what you are putting in your development plan. Now, this doesn't mean that you have to be able to fund or pay for everything today. You have to know that if your company doesn't support your learning, you would still want that opportunity.

Personal development and growth do directly benefit the company that you work for, and I believe in investing in my team members. If we don't invest in the team's growth, we are putting the company at risk. Henry Ford said, "The only thing worse than training your employees and having them leave is not training them and having them stay." Personal development is critical to increasing your value and impact in the workforce. Employees wishing to have continued career advancement should value learning and personal growth. Since you are reading this book, I assume you agree and already value personal development.

BUILDING YOUR PLAN, DAYS FOURTEEN TO SIXTEEN (THREE HOURS): PERSONAL DEVELOPMENT AND GROWTH PLAN

1. Identify the two to four areas that you want to develop over the next year that align with the company's goals.
2. Research learning opportunities.
3. Sort your ideas by category and type up your one-page Personal Development and Growth Plan by areas of learning. You do not need to list the financial investment but should have researched it.
4. Ask yourself the Big Question for each item. Are you willing to pay for the training if your company doesn't cover the investment?
5. Review the plan to ensure that your growth opportunities are in line with the company goals.

PRAYER

Dear Heavenly Father, I thank You for Your never-ending love. I thank You for helping me to identify areas of personal development that will help me to grow. Lord Jesus, I want to continue to grow to continue to be prepared to do Your will. Sometimes

I feel unqualified and doubt my abilities, Lord, but today I surrender to You, Lord, and ask You to guide the pen with which I write. I love You, Lord, Jesus, and I'm grateful for Your help. In Your Holy Name, I pray. Amen.

CHAPTER 22

SALARY RESEARCH

I was recently surfing through Facebook posts, and I came across an office assistant who asked if she should ask for a raise. Her office was getting ready to hire a new team member, and she caught wind that the new person coming in was asking for two dollars more per hour than she was currently making.

I knew I wanted to help this person. Her pay was so low I was shocked that she had worked at that rate for years. She justified why she should be paid so little. She lived in a small town, she liked her job, she liked her manager, and her husband earned enough for them to live. Sadly, she didn't know how to value herself. She thought she should ask now because she recently had some additional training and didn't feel it was fair for someone new to make more money.

When looking up the salary range in her area, I discovered she was underpaid by more than three dollars per hour, regardless of another team member being hired. That's $6,240 per year that she should have been making for being a great employee.

Knowing your value in the job market is wise; it allows you to understand the going rate for your position in your area and the country. Once you know the market value of your position, you can use these figures when negotiating your salary.

> OFTEN, WE FEAR NEGOTIATING, THINKING THAT WE WILL UPSET OUR BOSS OR MISS OUT ON A JOB OPPORTUNITY. THE TRUTH IS THAT THOSE WHO NEGOTIATE ARE OFTEN SEEN AS MORE COMPETENT AND ARE EVEN MORE SOUGHT AFTER.

Most employers won't tell you this, but they don't want you to leave, especially if you are the hardworking ones making a difference for the company. It's safe to assume that employee retention is even more important to the owner if you work in a smaller company or a startup.

This holds true for large organizations and small businesses. One of the top stressors for an entrepreneur and manager is finding and keeping great team members. More than anything, they don't want a revolving door of people.

It takes a tremendous amount of time and effort to hire and train someone new. Leaders often feel so threatened by team members leaving that they won't fire underperforming members due to the extra work and stress this causes. By knowing the market value for your position, you can communicate this to your manager as a form of negotiating. It's much like buying a car. Knowing the Kelly Blue Book value of a particular car provides the information you need to negotiate for a better price.

The average for your position in the job market is the lowest wage you should accept for your time and work. Why? Because you can reasonably go out into the job market and find a job making that amount of money. To find your job market worth, use a couple of websites. Go to www.GodsNotDoneWithYouBook.com/bonus to access the links. Do the same research on both sites, and then average the data. It's important to understand that these websites generate their data based on the information that people have provided. It's not a 100 percent full scope, and the data should be taken as information and not a limit to what you can and should be earning.

Go to the first website and type in your current position and the area in which you live. If you live in a small town, you can pick the city that is the closest drive to you. A salary amount will appear, and this is your average salary for your current position. You will also notice a graph that shows the range. Take note of the high end of the range. Next, complete the same search, but on a national basis. Take note of the averages and the ranges for your current position.

Next, go to the second website and repeat the same searching process for your current position in your area. Note the average and the top end of the range of the position. Then complete the same search, but on a national basis. Write down the averages and range again. You can take an average of the two averages to understand what your position pays today. If you are under the average and have been in your role or are excelling at your role, then you can ask for a raise and use the averages as a marker that you can go out into the job market and reasonably earn more today.

If you are making more than the average, this is excellent news. Being paid above the average is not a problem because you are actually seen as more valuable in the job market. Now that you know your current position market rate, you will want to find the rate of your desired position. You will complete the same process with the new title that you desire. Once you have all of the figures, find the average. This is the average for the new position.

Be sure to write this information down to either make it a part of your plan or have the information front of mind.

This is one area where you can decide how you want to present your request for compensation in the plan. If you make more than the average in your area, then you will not list the average in your plan. If you are making more than the national average, then you will not list it in your plan.

As I said, this is not a bad problem to have. You are likely a high-achieving team member that has been valued over the years. In many companies, people wear a lot of hats, and those unique skillsets have a tremendous amount of value. You are not average. Especially not now that you are helping to make a plan to help your company strategically. The amount of value that you will add compared to the standard disengaged team member is incredible. Always look to move yourself to the higher end of the range. You will focus more on growth and getting to the higher end of the range over trying to get to the average number for your compensation request.

If, on the other hand, you are not making more than the average for your current role and the role you desire, then you can include them in your plan. Your research shows the employer that you did your homework and are underpaid for your position in your market. If you are a great employee, they will feel the need to pay you more to keep you. Remember, the majority of business owners and managers do not want to lose their employees. They want you to talk to them and let them know what you desire.

FREQUENTLY ASKED QUESTIONS ABOUT COMPENSATION

I can't find information on my position. What can I do?

If the websites do not have enough data to compile reports, then you can talk to friends or colleagues outside of the company in similar roles to see what they are making. Don't limit your search by gender because you'll inevitably arrive at a lower salary than your male counterparts.

If you don't know anyone, you can connect with people on LinkedIn or join a Facebook group for your industry and ask in the private group.

If you have a trusted mentor/sponsor at work, you can ask what salary range they believe you should be earning for your position.

You can ask to have a private conversation with someone you trust in HR and ask them if you should be making more or to provide a range for your desired position. When asking, talk about position titles, not individuals.

My company has set salary ranges, and I'm at the top of my range. What should I do?

First, seek a promotion by completing a My Promotion Plan.

Don't think that this means that you still can't make more.

Many people make more than the top of their salary range and continue to get raises year after year. Even if it's 3 percent to cover the cost of living increases, what you don't ask for, you are less likely to get. Never forget that.

The new position that I want pays less than my current position. What should I do?

In this case, I don't recommend placing the salary average for the new position in your plan. The job market average isn't the only factor that determines your worth. You have a unique skillset, and adding to those skills makes you uniquely you.

Often, my clients are the ones that can improve efficiencies and grow their capacity, which means that they can do a lot of the responsibilities that they had before while taking on new tasks. This is great because you provide a maximum amount of value.

You are freeing up the owner's or manager's time. If the new role you desire to go into takes the load off of the owner or your manager, they will see this as more valuable.

TIME IS THE ONLY COMMODITY
THAT WE CAN'T BUY MORE OF.

Most business owners are thrilled when they can take more vacations while their business still makes money. Be that person, and you will become even more valuable.

BUILDING YOUR PLAN, DAY SEVENTEEN (ONE HOUR): SALARY RESEARCH

1. Use at least two resources to find your current position's range and average salary.
2. Use at least two resources to find your future position's range and average salary.

Links to websites can be found at www.GodsNotDoneWithYouBook.com/bonus.

PRAYER

Dear Heavenly Father, I thank You for allowing me to use technology with ease. Lord, I ask that You help me be confident in my value as I research what the world says about my position's value. Lord Jesus, I know that this value the world gives me does not determine the value You place on me. No matter the results, I know that You are my Ultimate Provider and Source. I ask You, Jesus, to help me remain surrendered to You and know that I am made of the most incredible value in Your eyes. I love You, Lord Jesus, and I'm grateful for Your help and never-ending love. In Your Holy Name, I pray. Amen.

CHAPTER 23

CLOSING AND POLISHING YOUR PLAN

CLOSING

People may skim the middle of a document, but they always read the beginning and the end. The closing is used to convey a final word of thanks and appreciation, ask for a promotion, and start the compensation conversation.

The closing is one to two paragraphs. You can think of it as the summary at the end of a chapter in a book. You hit the most important points.

When expressing thanks in the closing, frame it around the time spent reading the proposal and the opportunity to have a conversation. To make it more personal, include the names of your managers.

Since you have already laid out your ideas and strategy for the next position you desire, now is the time for you to let your manager know what position you would like. Be clear in what you are seeking and why you want this opportunity. Tie your skillsets into the sentence as an argument as to why you are perfect for this position.

Finally, include an ask for compensation or a request to talk about compensation. Everyone that you talk to will have a different opinion about whether you should ask for compensation. It's important that you express your desire to grow and earn more. Since you have done your salary research, you know what your current and future positions are worth in the job market.

Here are two ways to ask for compensation in the close:

1. List the position and the averages/range. Include the date and the source of your searches.
2. Request to talk about compensation without listing a specific number. This will allow your managers to make you an offer first, with you prepared to share the amount that you would like, having done your due diligence.

You should pick the option that feels most comfortable to you.

I don't recommend listing a specific compensation number that you are looking for. When you pick a number, you run the risk of selecting a number lower than your manager would have offered or selecting a number out of their budget, which distracts them from the overall value your plan provides.

In option number one, be sure only to include information that is helpful to your case. Do not put a range on the paper that you are not ok with earning the lower end of. Anytime you provide your employer with a range, assume that they will go at the low end.

When you provide a number, it acts as an anchor. In negotiations, the first number given is the anchor, and all other negotiations are done in context to that number. It doesn't mean that because two websites say that you should make X amount of dollars, your company will give you a 40K raise. They could do that, and I wouldn't discourage you from believing in a large raise; people do get raises of 40K and more.

At the same time, don't be shocked if, by placing a high anchor with context, you earn a 10 to 20 percent raise.

With option two, you leave yourself open to having a meaningful conversation around your compensation at the end of your meeting, which is why I've always been more comfortable with this option.

Your goal isn't to give your manager an ultimatum but to open the conversation to help you advance in your career.

WHEN YOU CAN START TO EXPRESS WHAT YOU WANT, YOU CAN BEGIN TO GET THE FEEDBACK NEEDED TO LEARN HOW TO GET TO THE NEXT POINT IN YOUR CAREER.

Once you have taken the time to write your closing, re-read the section aloud and ensure that you're communicating clearly, directly, and positively. Don't expect that your manager will be able to read your mind about what you want in a promotion or compensation increase. After reviewing yourself, review with a trusted friend or family member to get a second opinion. If they provide feedback beyond what is needed, that's ok, but understand that you do not have to take or use their feedback.

POLISHING

Imagine two gifts are sitting on a table. The contents of the packages are identical.

One is wrapped in a brown paper bag and is disheveled, and the other is perfectly wrapped with gold and red glitter wrapping. The gold and red glitter package has a large bow and a card attached.

If you were given one of these presents from a friend, which would you perceive is more valuable? The disheveled bag or the carefully wrapped package?

Of course, the perfectly wrapped package would hold a higher perceived value.

To enhance the promotion plan, design a cover page that gets the proper attention. Early on, you should have developed a theme for the promotion plan. The cover page is the perfect place to introduce the theme and set the promotion plan's tone.

As you start to consider the design of the cover page, align it with your company or something that your manager is fond of if you can relate it to your theme. Use the company's logo and colors to keep it cohesive with the brand.

If you don't have a copy of the logo or know the HEX numbers of the company colors, you can ask someone in the media or marketing department for your company's brand guide. Many smaller companies won't have a brand guide. Check with the person in charge of HR for any details that they may have and to understand if any usage rules apply.

Include the following items on your cover page: your name, company name or logo, theme, the date, and a photo/abstract image.

There are many options for the cover page, and you should choose the option that works best for you.

1. Use Microsoft Word to create a simple cover page. Select a new template and choose a format that speaks to you.
2. Use a free online design service and create your custom cover page in no time. Visit www.GodsNotDoneWithYouBook.com/bonus for links to my recommended sites.
3. Use an in-house graphic designer to create a cover page for you.

Once you have completed your plan, it's time to complete a grammar check. Start by proofreading your entire plan. Next, you can use a free online resource to help you with any finishing touches. You can do a Google search to find the latest tools or my latest recommendation on the resource website.

If you want a more thorough grammar check, then enlist a friend or family member who's skilled in this area to help you.

Once you have completed the grammar check, it is time to format your promotion plan. Start on page one and ensure that the first page consists only of the appreciation letter. The second page will start with your accomplishments. Using a service like Google Docs or Microsoft Word, you can easily format items, using bullet points or a numerical system. The key is to keep the formatting consistent throughout the project.

Check the page breaks and ensure that new accomplishments or ideas start on a new page. This may extend the document by three or four pages, but it will be well worth it if the information is more easily digestible.

For the sections, come up with creative names that match the theme of your promotion plan. For example, the accomplishments section could be called "Previous Objectives Completed," "Value Add Accomplishments From 20XX," or "Relentlessly Driving Success." If you are creative in this area, let yourself have fun. If not, any heading will work; don't overthink it. The value truly lies within the sections.

Next, add in a header and a footer. Include the company logo, page numbers, the theme of the plan, and your name. If the header or footers have color, ensure that they are in line with the company colors.

Once you have completed the cover page, grammar check, and formatting, it's time to print and bind your promotion plan. Print your promotion plan in color and on nice paper. You will want to print one copy for each person receiving the plan and a copy for yourself.

If you can print and bind the promotion plans in your office, this would be acceptable since the promotion plan enhances the company. If you cannot print and bind in your office, I recommend using a local or nationwide office supply store to print and bind.

Many office supply stores provide store purchasing discount cards for companies. You can check with the finance department to see if your company has one. The card can be used to get a discount for printing and binding. If you have an out-of-pocket expense, this expense is on you as an investment in your future.

Ensure that your document is final before taking it to have it print and bound. Don't skimp in this area. It can make all of the difference when you go to turn in your promotion plan.

The finishing details are not what will get you the promotion, but it will further set you apart from others and present your ideas in the best possible way.

Once you have the plans ready to print, you will want to double-check calendars. The date you will be turning your plan in is coming up, and you want to ensure that your appointment to review your plan is still on the calendar.

Once you know that your meeting is on the calendar, start printing.

Congratulations! You have completed your promotion plan. Now it's time to prepare for your promotion meeting.

BUILDING YOUR PLAN, DAYS EIGHTEEN TO TWENTY-TWO (FIVE HOURS): CLOSING AND POLISHING YOUR PLAN

1. Pick one of the two options and write your closing paragraph. (Plant an anchor in your closing if using option one.)
2. Decide if you will make a salary report part of your promotion plan.
3. Have a trusted friend review your closing, and ask them if it's clear that you want a promotion and higher compensation.

4. Create a cover page that matches your theme, company culture, and company colors.
5. Complete a grammar check. For an online tool, visit www.GodsNotDoneWithYouBook.com/bonus.
6. Add in titles for the different sections.
7. Format headers, footers, and page breaks.
8. Print in color and professionally bind (one copy per person in the meeting, including yourself).
9. Double-check that your career advancement meeting is still on the calendar.

PRAYER

Dear Heavenly Father, You are Jehovah-Nissi, The Lord, my Banner. I thank You for allowing me to complete the My Promotion Plan. I thank You for Your help with technology today. Lord, I ask that You help me to remain confident and excited as I polish my plan. I thank You for Your love and guidance through this process. Lord, I ask that You help me to be confident in asking to increase my compensation. May I always trust in You and Your promises. Lord Jesus, I surrender to You, and I ask for the words I should place in this closing statement. May these words convey my love for the company, my managers, and my desire to grow my potential. I love You, Lord Jesus, and I'm grateful for Your help and never-ending love. In Your Holy Name. Amen.

CHAPTER 24

PREPARING YOURSELF, PRESENTING YOUR PLAN, AND OWNING YOUR MEETING

PREPARATION

Now that your plan is polished and printed, it's time to prepare for your career advancement meeting and turn in your plan. Through your Daily Mind Renewal Routine, you have been reprogramming your mind, body, and heart. You are feeling better than ever before. In this chapter, you'll learn about additional tools that you can use on the day of your career advancement meeting. We'll look at how to build your confidence even more to help you stay relaxed in your meeting.

First, remember that you're not in this alone. Take more time to pray, read your Bible, meditate, and get into nature. Reflect on the promises that God says are already yours.

If you start to doubt yourself, your ability, or your worth, remember that God doesn't make junk. He made you uniquely you and has brought you to this moment. He takes delight in you and does not want you to fear or worry.

God never leaves or forsakes you. He is quite literally with you always, so speak to Him and tell Him your heart's desires. I like to picture God sitting with me, riding in the passenger seat of my car, and walking around with me at my office. He is there, no matter what the situation is or where we are. God is with us.

> ISAIAH 41:10 SAYS, "SO DO NOT FEAR, FOR I AM WITH YOU; DO NOT BE DISMAYED, FOR I AM YOUR GOD. I WILL STRENGTHEN YOU AND HELP YOU; I WILL UPHOLD YOU WITH MY RIGHTEOUS RIGHT HAND."

Here are some practical steps to consider as you prepare to get in the right frame of mind and raise your frequency.

- Confidence is manifest in the body. As you approach your meeting day, carry yourself with a posture that reflects your faith in God and in yourself. Don't be closed off and reserved. Hold yourself high with an openness to your future opportunity.
- Listening to music is a great way to instill calm and increase confidence. Find the songs that speak to you. I recommend praise and worship music that is meditative, so you're aligning your preparation for career success with God's plan for your life.
- Another confidence and frequency boost can come from using essential oils. Choose an essential oil with a scent that will bring you to a place of relaxation. I've been using Young

Living Essential Oils for several years and highly recommend them. Two of my favorites are lavender and Stress Away.

- Feeling good about your clothing has been linked to increased confidence. Take time to go shopping and outfit yourself so you feel fabulous in your meeting. I like to have two outfits ready to go. One for the day I turn in My Promotion Plan and one for the day of the meeting. The key is to feel comfortable, be professional, and wear material that is breathable. You know you have the right outfit when you put it on and feel like a million dollars!
- If you wear jewelry, I suggest picking pieces that have powerful meaning for you. I often wear a cross necklace or a heart necklace with an "M" in it that my grandmother gave me that reminds me of her and of God's presence with me.

With all these things in place, two other things that can help you prepare are roleplay and additional visualizations.

Roleplay is practicing the meeting as if it is happening with another person. Pick one or two people you trust, wear your million-dollar outfit, and take them through your plan. This will give you a chance to work through any parts that still need improvement, identify moments you haven't fully developed, or work through any parts of the meeting that feel stressful when you look into the future.

Visualization is another exercise that allows you to get extra practice when you don't have a partner to roleplay with. Find a quiet space and close your eyes. Bring yourself to a state of awareness by focusing on each of your senses. Then start to visualize your career advancement meeting day. Picture yourself in your office, calm and confident, wearing your million-dollar outfit, walking down the hallway, sitting in your meeting, and holding your promotion plan. Picture the room around you, feel the confident smile on your face, and work your way through the career advancement meeting. Visualize your feelings of confidence and excitement and the positive responses from your manager. Go through your ideas and visualize your manager liking your ideas, asking questions, and expressing excitement. Then imagine reviewing your personal growth and development plan. Finally, visualize asking for a promotion with confidence and an increase in compensation. See the smile on your face and the positive reactions of your manager. Visualize talking about the salary that you desire and working through the negotiation. Visualize yourself telling a loved one about the advancement that you have received.

TURNING IN YOUR PLAN

You've built your plan, and the time has come to turn it in and have your career advancement meeting. The day before the meeting, be sure to submit your printed and professionally bound promotion plan. Let your manager know that you have time on the schedule the following day to review a few ideas for the company.

When you turn in your plan, most managers will be so intrigued that they will read it straight away. It's rare, but your manager could feel as though they don't have time to review your plan before the meeting the next day. If your manager expresses a lack of time to be prepared, let them know that you would like to review the main idea section with them during the meeting, and there is nothing they need to have ready.

If they don't have time to review your plan, be prepared to summarize the contents so that they hear from you what they would have read in the appreciation letter, your list of accomplishments, and your ideas for company growth.

OWNING YOUR MEETING

If you can, clear your schedule for the fifteen to thirty minutes before your meeting to go through any last-minute confidence boosters and a short meditation. You want to stay focused on the goals of your meeting: asking for a raise or promotion, getting the green light on your ideas for rapid implementation, and receiving support for your personal and career advancement plans moving forward.

For your meeting to go well, start off by building rapport. Stay upbeat and friendly. Smiling is contagious, and your emotional energy and body language will transfer to your manager. Again, it's natural to be nervous, but you will likely notice that you are not nearly as nervous as you expected.

YOU'VE PREPARED FOR THIS. YOU'RE READY.

Remember that and adjust your posture if you find yourself fidgeting, doodling, placing your hand on your face or neck, or hair-twirling.

Lead with gratitude. Take time to thank your manager(s) for taking the time to meet with you, and express how much you enjoy working at the company.

Stay on time and stay on task as you go through your plan with them. Allow time for your manager to ask questions, and be prepared for some pushback. It's to be expected that your manager won't like every idea. That's ok. This is not a time to argue or fight for the things that you want; it's the time to show that you've given real thought to your company's growth and your contribution to it. Accentuate the positive and be attentive to your manager's concerns that might strengthen your own ideas.

Once you've shared your ideas, it's time to connect that to your personal development and growth plan. Take time to talk about how and why you want to grow, gauge your manager's support, and see if there's a budget for personal development training. Be sure to express how this will add value to the company and not only yourself. Every company is different. But ask with confidence and believe it will happen. Those individuals within the organization that are learning and growing are the ones that will continue to advance. The more visible your growth, the more others will trust you and look up to you.

Then it's time to review your desired position and ask for a promotion. Again, be confident, lead with gratitude, trust your ideas, and ask for the position that you want. Once you've done all this, the ball will be in your manager's court. They will talk to you about the position and the compensation. Here are four typical scenarios.

1. They will ask you what you want to be paid. You've done your research. So you should have a number in mind. Don't shortchange yourself.
2. They will offer you a raise and give you a specific number. Unless the numbers are unexpectedly high, be prepared to negotiate.
3. They will tell you that there isn't any money in the budget to accommodate your request. If your company has been struggling, this could likely be the case. You should still ask for what you want and can always ask for benefits that are

not compensation related. This will help set future expectations. You can always ask for another review after ninety days to talk about compensation based on company growth or inquire about having your raise go into effect the next time budgets are set.

4. They will throw you a curveball and talk to you about your performance. This isn't common, but if they have concerns about your performance, they will have a hard time increasing your pay. They may offer suggestions about areas where you can improve. If this happens, be receptive and show that you're open to feedback. Then schedule regular meetings to review your performance and ask to have another meeting in three to six months. This is the feedback that you have needed all along to help your manager see that you are right for the next position.

BUILDING YOUR PLAN, DAYS TWENTY-THREE TO TWENTY-SIX (EIGHT HOURS): PREPARING YOURSELF, PRESENTING YOUR PLAN, AND OWNING YOUR MEETING

1. Select and practice the confidence boosters you want to use.
2. Pick out your million-dollar outfit and an outfit to wear the day you turn in your plan.
3. Spend extra time in prayer, meditation, and worship to stay focused on what you want.
4. Practice your career advancement meeting as many times as possible (at minimum, three times).
5. Visualize your career advancement meeting daily.
6. Have your career advancement meeting.

Go to www.GodsNotDoneWithYouBook.com/bonus to learn more about essential oils and to gain access to my pre-career advancement playlist.

PRAYER

Dear Heavenly Father, I thank You for Your never-ending, never-failing love and kindness. Lord, I ask that You help me remain confident and excited as I prepare to turn in my plan. Thank You for keeping my mind and thoughts focused on You, and I pray for a positive outcome in my career advancement meeting if it is Your will. Lord, there are sometimes thoughts that come into my mind that create doubt. I know that these are not from You, and I ask that You give me Your grace to keep my eyes and heart focused on only serving Your will. I thank You for Your love and guidance through this process. I love You, Lord, Jesus. In Your Holy Name, Amen.

DAY OF CAREER ADVANCEMENT MEETING PRAYER

Dear Heavenly Father, You are Jehovah-Shammah, and I'm grateful that You are here with me today. I thank You for Your never-ending, never-failing love and kindness. Lord Jesus, thank You for bringing me to this point. I surrender to You, Lord. I ask that You help me to remain confident and excited as I have my career advancement meeting. I pray that You enter into my manager's heart and help them be open and accepting of my ideas. I ask that You send me extra guardian angels and that You would shield me from any thoughts of doubt. Knowing that whatever happens in the meeting, I will praise You all the same, may Your Kingdom come and Your will be done. Lord, I thank You for going before me to make a path and for always standing right with me. To You, Lord Jesus, I give all of the praise. I love You, Lord. In Your Holy Name, Amen.

CHAPTER 25

LIFE AFTER YOUR CAREER ADVANCEMENT MEETING

Every person that I've seen complete a promotion plan experiences exponential growth after turning in the plan. But as I shared in the previous chapter, there are four possibilities coming out of the career advancement meeting. Always be confident in a positive outcome to your career advancement meeting, even though it's unrealistic to think that it will be a perfect bed of roses every time. What you do after the meeting is most important.

The majority of people will land the promotion or will be told to start working toward the promotion. If this is you, congratulations! Take time to thank God for your success. One of my favorite parts of earning a raise is the ability to give more away. You should celebrate and do something kind for yourself too.

If you didn't get the result you were looking for, this is a good time to reflect. This book focuses on the things that women can do to advocate for themselves. But there's no doubt that discrimination in the workplace still exists, and it's possible that this can contribute to a negative outcome. If you feel that you are being treated unfairly because you are a woman, take time to talk to God and listen for His guidance. If needed, talk to a trusted advisor and plan a course of action. You always have the choice to change careers and find another place that values you.

If you don't feel it was discrimination, set a follow-up meeting to ask for advice on how you can advance within the company. Having open dialogue allows you to understand what the company needs and how you can fill those roles. Take time to reflect on the experience and whatever feedback you can act on to improve your performance. This is when you prove that you have what it takes or become defeated and do nothing. Take what you can from the meeting and put it into action.

One way or another, now it's time to get to work. The perfect promotion plan is pointless if you don't execute. Start by reviewing your plan and setting your priorities in light of your manager's feedback. Also, think about your teammates and the people you lead if you have a team. Your promotion plan and priorities will have a major impact on them too. As you climb the ladder, you need to focus more on strategy and ensure that you implement the ideas that will have the largest return on investment.

As you work through your new projects in your new position, be open to change, but don't lose complete focus on the ideas that got you to this position. It's not uncommon for some of your proposed ideas not to work out. But you don't want to look back at the end of a year and realize that you didn't act on your plan. Take time to reflect and evaluate monthly on how your progress is. What is going well? What is not going so well?

At the end of a project, reflect on the process. How could you have made the implementation easier? What lessons did you learn as a result of this project? Did you achieve the desired outcome(s)? Can you take it up a notch or make improvements? Has the team bought in? Is this now a standard part of your company?

Leading with these questions will show your manager and colleagues that you're committed to more than your own promotion. You're a leader with the ability to learn and grow, which will help you become one of your company's most valuable assets. Keep track of your progress, and remember that learning is a journey, not a race. Enjoy the journey in flow.

Once you know the promotion planning process, earning promotions or raises year after year becomes more comfortable. If you keep track of your achievements, ideas/challenges that need to be solved, and how you want to continue to grow along the way, now you're creating your plan as you go. When a year comes around, or a promotion opportunity opens up, type up your plan, and you are ready to go.

If you're like most women who create promotion plans, you want to leave a legacy.

BY CREATING AND TURNING IN YOUR PROMOTION PLAN, YOU ARE PART OF HISTORY, AND YOUR SUCCESS WILL BE AN EXAMPLE FOR OTHER WOMEN TO FOLLOW.

Zig Ziglar says, "You can have everything you want in life if you will just help other people get what they want."[109] Many women complete their promotion plans and want to share the process with their teams. Why? First, they become empowered through the process and want others around them to reach their full potential. Second, they believe in their team and know that they also have ideas to make the workplace better and that will grow the company. Great leaders know the power of an engaged team.

True fulfillment in life will never be gained through our own successes. The true fulfillment and joy in life is when we can help encourage, lead, and empower others. John C. Maxwell says it's when we move from success to significance. I wish you much success, and I pray that you would value others as much as you do yourself and find ways always to add value to others so that you can experience the joys of significance.

In our Inner Circle Mastermind group, we teach you how to help your team create "Power Plans," which are similar to promotion plans. When the team is engaged, everyone wins. Taking time to nurture and grow your team is how you can leave a legacy and touch many hearts and lives. Maya Angelou said, "I've learned that people will forget what you said, people will forget what you did, but people will never forget how you made them feel."[110]

As you grow as a leader and develop as an executive, do everything you can to help others gain confidence and have opportunities. When we work together, we can change history and write a new story for future generations.

Never forget that you were created with divine power for greatness. Never forget to claim your value. Never forget what God says about you. As you continue this journey, you will experience more and more of what God has promised and already given you. Before long, others will start to notice the difference in you, and everything will become easier. Not because anything changed within the world but because you now see the world through a different lens.

My prayer for you is that your mind would be renewed, allowing your heart to be fertile soil for the love of Jesus to grow and that you would have the peace of God, which surpasses all understanding, and that you will guard your hearts and your minds in Christ Jesus forever.[111]

God's Not Done with You!

CONCLUSION

Are you willing to help change the history of future generations of women?

You are now equipped with the knowledge to change the statistics and write the history of our future. When you believe in yourself, you can climb higher than you ever dreamed possible. Take time daily to take care of your body and mind. When we have the right thinking, we are capable of anything.

Everything you need is in this book.

My sincere hope is that you take action by making a promotion plan and transform your career and life. That you embrace the covenant that God has made with you through Jesus and that God becomes your best friend. That you continue to feed your mind through meditation, prayer, gratitude, and affirmations, allowing you to continue to peel off each layer of the onion that has been trapping the greatness within you.

The future generations of women are counting on you as a role model to believe that they too can do it.

Right now, you have your plan in your hand that will forever change your company and your life. With each profound moment in our lives, we stand at a crossroads. We choose to continue on the same path or decide to do something different.

We all have to make a choice, which can be scary.

Don't be scared! Now is your time to choose the life you want to live.

When you believe in yourself and make a promotion plan, I know your future can be transformed into anything you desire.

I hope by this point that you believe in yourself and your abilities. If you don't, you can borrow my belief in you. I believe you are made for more and that God has planned a prosperous future for you.

You deserve to get that promotion to stay on track with all your career goals.

You deserve to get that promotion to feel confident that you are living to your fullest potential.

You deserve to get that promotion to live the life of peace and prosperity you've been dreaming of.

You deserve to get that promotion.

Many women like to share their stories of success, and I'd love to hear yours. You can connect with me on social media and by email at mary@mypromotionplan.com. Or subscribe to my blog at www.MaryGuirovich.com/Podcast.

I'd love for you to share this book with other women if you find it valuable. I'm on a mission to help people love the work they do so we can experience work as worship as God originally intended it. The world has changed and is continuing to change, and together we can champion today's working women to believe in themselves, allowing them to dream bigger. I envision a world where a woman with influence sits at every table as we work to improve workplace cultures and eradicate the gender parity gap. If more women know God's love and advance into leadership positions across the world, then we can change what future generations of girls believe is possible for them and their careers.

Believe. Plan. Transform.

God's Not Done with You!

With Love,

Mary

P.S. If you haven't yet accepted Jesus as your Lord and Savior, I invite you to by saying the prayer of salvation found in the Appendix. Believing in Jesus is not enough, even Satan believes in Him. We must personally accept Him as Lord in our lives.

ACKNOWLEDGMENTS

First and foremost, I thank God for creating me and providing me with the opportunity to encourage other women through promotion planning. Without God, none of this would have been possible.

I'm thankful for my clients who have put their trust in me as they have worked to advance their careers. Your testimonies helped keep me going on the days when the editing became challenging. Thank you for getting on the group calls and getting vulnerable when asking questions.

There have been many women who have written about women's career advancement or have openly advocated for women that have inspired me: Dr. Linda Babcock, Sara Laschever, Joanne Lipman, Rachel Hollis, Dr. Stefanie K. Johnson, Kay White, Katelyn Beaty, Mel Robbins, J.D., Helen Mitchell, and Cheryl Bachelder. These women have stood up for equality in the workplace for women, are encouraging women to step up, and are actively engaged in changing the traditional workplace culture. Although we've never spoken, your books, courses, blogs, research, and videos have been a blessing as I have worked to more fully understand the many challenges that so many women face across the globe when it comes to women stepping up into leadership roles.

Mary Barra, although we have never met, you have inspired me through your role at GM while advocating for women. I'm so grateful for your willingness to take time to help other women advance. It is because of women like you and Sheryl Sandberg that I gained confidence to press forward in my career while starting to speak out to help other women.

Sheryl Sandberg, I thank you for writing *Lean In*. It was the first text that I read years ago that made me feel like I wasn't alone and the workplace could, in fact, improve to be more equitable for women.

Many people have made the exploration of quantum physics, meditation, self-awareness, the mind, and energy healing both exciting and understandable: Dr. Bruce Lipton, Dr. Joe Dispenza, Dr. Daniel Amen, Jim Kwick, Gary Craig, Dr. Richard Hawkins, Dr. Martin Rossman, Dr. Dawson Church, Dr. Maxwell Maltz, and Emily Fletcher. Thank you for your research, work, and dedication that has changed my life and the lives of so many others.

To Jennifer Allwood, Pete Vargas, Pedro Ado, and Dr. Bradley Nelson for your research and work, but more importantly for sharing your faith with your message. You have each inspired me to confidently share my faith.

Thank you to Tauren Wells and Micah Tyler. Micah, your song "Different" has been my personal anthem. Even after listening to it every day for years, it still moves me powerfully. I'll never forget the Sunday in November when you sang at CBC, it was the hope I needed. Tauren, I have shed many tears of hope listening to your song "God's Not Done with You" as I took hard steps in my life. When working to name the book, I had one of those hard days and I was singing your song. That's when I knew what God wanted women to know, He's not done with them.

There have been many other people that have believed in me, encouraged me, and have helped me to grow into the woman I am today, making the dream of writing this book into a reality.

Laura Ann Christman, I thank you for luring me with pancakes to The Bible Chapel. To Pastor Ron Moore, who preached the message the day I accepted Jesus into my heart. To my early friends at the church: Boyd, Carl, Tony, Kelly, Tim, Meghan, Leah, Dan, Mariann, and Derreck for helping me to know Christ.

A huge thank you to the Scribe Tribe for making the process of writing and editing a book as enjoyable as possible. A special thanks to Emily Gindlesparger, Hal Clifford, Chas Hoppe, Hussein Al-Baiaty, and Drew Appelbaum for your weekly guidance and encouragement.

To my project managers Rose Friel and Neddie Ann Underwood for answering my countless questions and keeping my book publishing on track. Thank you to the gifted Teresa Muñiz for designing the most radiantly beautiful book cover. Mariano Paniello, you made the book come to life with the beautiful graphics. It was pure joy to see images take on a beautiful feminine presence.

To my brilliant editor Robert L. Kehoe III, for embracing the essence of my writing while making the text more concise and clear. May you be blessed for being so caring, gentle, and encouraging.

To the talented Linda Wright, Norma Brown, Natalia Pagán Serrano, Geoff Pope, and Samantha Hendrix, who helped to ensure that all the details were worked out and God's word was preserved. From the moment God told me He was supposed to be in my book, my biggest goal was to ensure I honored Him and His word by representing it accurately. I believe that He divinely connected us.

To Amber Vilhauer, the NGNG Team, Jess Hershey, and the MOCA team for being a creative and strategic marketing force for my book and brand. I can't thank you enough for believing in my mission and building my platform so women across the globe can be empowered.

A huge thank you to my mentors Dr. Helen McCracken and Mark Cole, who have patiently and honestly believed, taught, coached, and encouraged me to a higher potential. Because of each of you, I have experienced breakthroughs that have transformed my ability to serve others.

Dr. Jim Richards, thank you for encouraging me to experience God and to live my life as a disciple. Your stories, books, and teachings have greatly encouraged and aided me to know God more and to understand the vastness of His love.

To my friend and mentor, John C. Maxwell, thank you for listening to God's will for your life many years ago. Because of you and The John Maxwell Team, I've been forever changed by your messages, books, and the mentors that you introduce us to. Your team helped me to learn how to take the limits off of my dreams so I can be a leader that focuses on encouraging others to reach heights they've never dreamed possible.

To the entire service team at Eggspectation in San Antonio, Texas, for always happily taking care of me. You are world-class. Thank you for allowing me to take the coveted corner booth all day on Saturday as I worked to write and edit this book. I'll always have fond memories of writing while drinking my hot chamomile tea.

Thank you to my high school English teacher, Mrs. Hatfield, for the opportunity to take college writing even though I was well below the standards needed. I'll never forget those yellow Post-It notes from the professor with their positive feedback. Although splashes of red filled my pages, your willingness to take a chance on me and give me loads of extra help gave me a seed of hope that allowed me to take that next step in believing I could learn to be a better writer.

Dr. Charlie Webb, I love you. Thank you for believing, challenging, listening, leading, and mentoring me for the last nine years. Your ability to always trust me and see my future potential drove me to continue to grow. Without your guidance and support, I wouldn't be the woman I am today.

Mindi Webb, thank you for hiring me to work at the Imagine Wellness Centre and for being a living example of Christ. Your ability to lead with love and accountability taught me more than you'll ever know. From the moment I heard you speak about the job opening, I knew that God wanted me near you.

Without this next person, my business wouldn't exist today. John, I'm grateful for the many years that we have had together. Each day is another lesson to learn from. Thank you for encouraging me to start a business and for challenging me each day to be the best version of myself.

Danielle, I'm so blessed to have a sister in Christ like you in life. You are incredible, and I'm so grateful for our weekly Bible study time when we can grow closer to Christ together. Thank you for being a graceful example of Christ's love. I love you!

To the rest of the FPC Team, each of you have left a mark on my heart. The way you each show up everyday day, taking extreme ownership to coach our clients to success is never taken for granted. You are making a difference in the world, and I feel blessed to have shared this journey with you. The truth is a leader can only be as great as their team, and you have made my time in leadership abundantly rewarding. We are changing ten million lives and revolutionizing healthcare.

FPC Family, so many of you had the opportunity to watch me grow into my role. Thank you for believing in me, trusting me, and encouraging me along the way. Because of your willingness to trust and have authentic conversations, it allowed me to understand what the clients wanted and needed to succeed at even higher levels. Having the opportunity to watch so many of you create the practice of your dreams has been inspiring. You are changing ten million lives!

To Pastor Dr. Ed Newton, who loves Jesus and isn't afraid to preach the truth and challenge us as a congregation to make disciples of ourselves. Every week I feel like you are talking to me. We are CBC, CBC are we! We are changing the world from San Antonio, TX. Thank you for speaking life into me as I grew into the disciple that God created me to be.

To my friends Amanda, Melischa, Kamille, Heather, Liz, Sofia, Yvette, and Abby, who supported me and listened to my book for hours. Your friendship and support sustain me. Thank you for your time, encouragement, and love.

Holly, you are the best friend that a girl could ever ask for. I love you so much, and I can't thank you enough for talking me off the ledge and reminding me to bet on myself—that and the many other lessons that life has taught us through adulting.

Thank you to each of my siblings, Vicki, R.J., and David, for supporting me in your own unique ways. I love you all so much, and I'm grateful to be your sister.

Without you, Mom and Dad, I wouldn't be here today. Thank you for putting me first, loving me unconditionally, believing in me, and supporting me in life—especially when I didn't believe in myself.

Grandma Becker, you are the best grandma in the world—so full of life, love, and gratitude. Thank you for asking weekly about my book on our calls and for your encouragement. You would always say that I made your day, but, Grandma, you made mine.

To my kids, Lauren, Ian, Emily, and Dalton, for supporting me in God's will and for sacrificing time with me and helping around the house so I could give to others. I love y'all so much, and I'm so blessed to be your mom. Never stop dreaming, always believe, and trust God to help guide you in life.

Saving the best for last, this book wouldn't be possible without my amazing husband, Louis. I love you! This book truly exists today because of your belief in me, your support of my crazy dream, and your love for our family. Thank you for taking the kids on Saturdays and for getting Dalton to school every day. Thank you for taking care of our home and for taking care of me. You love me in the most incredible way, and I'm blessed to be your wife.

APPENDIX

PRAYER OF SALVATION

If you want to put your faith and trust in Jesus today, call on His name. He came to rescue you. Let Him save you today. Call on His name and say this to Him:

Lord Jesus, I know that I'm not perfect, but I believe in You. Come into my heart, save me, and change me. I give You my life. Amen.

It's a simple as that. Romans 10:9–10 says, "If you confess with your mouth, 'Jesus is Lord,' and believe in your heart that God raised him from the dead, you will be saved. For it is with your heart that you believe and are justified, and it is with your mouth that you confess and are saved."

All of Heaven is celebrating today because of your choice. I'd love to celebrate with you too and have a small gift for you. To let me know, go to www.GodsNotDoneWithYouBook.com/bonus.

ABOUT THE AUTHOR

MARY E. GUIROVICH is the CEO and founder of My Promotion Plan (MPP), a company that empowers women to unlock their innate leadership potential and advance in their careers holistically. Over the course of her nearly twenty-year career, she has managed large teams, consulted with over thirty nationally recognized hospitality brands working with teams in hundreds of locations, has coached hundreds of medical practitioners and owners, trained thousands of team members, and helped to open and run two multimillion-dollar businesses.

But years ago, when Mary was floundering to earn a promotion she desperately wanted, God told her to make a plan. She approached her goals holistically and created a plan that extended beyond the immediate promotion she wanted, into a vision for her entire career. The day after she turned in her promotion plan, she was appointed Vice President of Operations.

Mary was soon named Chief Operating Officer and then a partner. She made the climb from a front-office position in only six years—with no prior experience in the industry. After experiencing success, she started teaching others her process, and they too earned promotions and raises in the 20 percent range. Mary started her online My Promotion Plan course so she could continue to support the needs of women across the country. The MPP process has an 83 percent customer success rate, helping members advance without waiting for their bosses to approach them. Mary's course has now been distilled in this book.

In addition to helping individual women, Mary partners with organizations and businesses that seek to educate and implement practices that create more equality, diversity, and inclusivity in their workplaces. In addition to her rich work history, Mary is certified as a consultant in DiSC, Another Seat At The Table (Diversity, Equity, and Inclusion), and Appreciation in the Workplace. A Certified John C. Maxwell Coach, Trainer, and Speaker, Mary was awarded the Willfully Grow Culture Award in 2020.

Mary is married to Louis and has four children, Lauren, Ian, Emily, and Dalton, and fur baby, Jack. The family belongs to Community Bible Church, and Mary serves on the CBC Cares Team. She lives in San Antonio, TX, where you will find her rocking out to country and Christian music, studying the Bible, throwing Pinterest parties, floating down the river, cooking for friends, and crafting with vinyl.

NOTES

1 Joanne Lipman, "Women Are Still Not Asking for Pay Rises. Here's Why," *World Economic Forum*, April 12, 2018, https://www.weforum.org/agenda/2018/04/women-are-still-not-asking-for-pay-rises-here-s-why/.

2 Claire Cain Miller, "The Motherhood Penalty vs. the Fatherhood Bonus," *The Upshot*, *The New York Times*, September 6, 2014, https://www.nytimes.com/2014/09/07/upshot/a-child-helps-your-career-if-youre-a-man.html.

3 Sylvia Ann Hewlett, "Executive Women and the Myth of Having It All," *Harvard Business Review*, April 2002, https://hbr.org/2002/04/executive-women-and-the-myth-of-having-it-all.

4 Oliver Burkeman, "Dirty Secret: Why Is There Still a Housework Gender Gap?" *The Guardian*, February 17, 2018, https://www.theguardian.com/inequality/2018/feb/17/dirty-secret-why-housework-gender-gap.

5 Clare Sebastian, "Why Women Pay More than Men for the Same Stuff," CNN Money, March 7, 2016, https://money.cnn.com/2016/03/07/pf/pink-tax/index.html.

6 "Equal Pay Counts: What Companies Can Do," LeanIn.Org, 2021, https://leanin.org/what-companies-can-do-about-equal-pay; Richard Fry, "U.S. Women Near Milestone in the College-educated Labor Force," Pew Research Center, June 20, 2019, https://pewrsr.ch/2ZEVQB3.

7 R. David Freedman, "Woman, a Power Equal to a Man: Translation of Woman as a 'Fit Helpmate' for Man Is Questioned," *Biblical Archaeology Review* 9, no. 1 (1983): 56–58, https://www.baslibrary.org/biblical-archaeology-review/9/1/6.

8 Jimena, "Ezer Kenegdo," *Ezer Kenegdo* (blog), February 22, 2018, https://ezerkenegdo.org/ezer-kenegdo/.

9 Carolyn Custis James, "The Ezer-Kenegd: Ezer Unleashed," FaithGateway, March 20, 2015, https://www.faithgateway.com/ezer-unleashed/#.YWjvXhDMI_V.

10 Sarah E. Fisher, "Valour: How Biblical Translation Has Failed the 'Chayil' Woman," *Hebrew Word Lessons* (blog), January 14, 2018, https://hebrewwordlessons.com/2018/01/14/valour-how-biblical-translation-has-failed-the-chayil-woman/; Judg. 6:12; Judg. 20:46; 1 Sam. 9:1a; 1 Chron. 5:18; Ezek. 37:3–6, 10; Ruth 3:11; Prov. 12:4; Prov. 31:10; Prov. 31:29 ESV.

11 Acts 16; Rom. 16; Acts 18.

12 Acts 18:2–3; Acts 18–19; Acts 26; Rom. 16:3–5; 1 Cor. 16–19; 2 Tim. 4:19.

13 Exod. 1; Josh. 2; Judg. 4–5; 2 Kings 22.

14 Judg. 4–5.

15 Barilla Taylor, "The Role of Women in the Industrial Revolution," Tsongas Industrial History Center, accessed August 8, 2021, https://www.uml.edu/tsongas/barilla-taylor/women-industrial-revolution.aspx.

16 Sara Horrell and Jane Humphries, "The Origins and Expansion of the Male Breadwinner Family: The Case of Nineteenth-century Britain," *International Review of Social History* 42 (September 1997): 25–64, https://doi.org/10.1017/s0020859000114786.

17 Kim England and Kate Boyer, "Women's Work: The Feminization and Shifting Meanings of Clerical Work," *Journal of Social History* 43, no. 2 (December 2009): 307–340. https://doi.org/10.1353/jsh.0.0284.

18 Elaine Tyler May, "Elaine Tyler May," PBS, accessed October 10, 2021, https://www.pbs.org/wgbh/americanexperience/features/tupperware-may/.

19 History.com Editors, "American Women in World War II," History.com, accessed October 10, 2021, https://www.history.com/topics/world-war-ii/american-women-in-world-war-ii-1.

20 May, "Elaine Tyler May."

21 Suyin Haynes, "The Global Gender Gap Will Take an Extra 36 Years to Close After the COVID-19 Pandemic, Report Finds," *Time*, March 30, 2021, https://time.com/5951101/global-gender-gap-135-years/.

22 "2019 Statistics: Women Onscreen," WomenandHollywood.com, accessed September 8, 2020, https://womenandhollywood.com/resources/statistics/2019-statistics/.

23 Rom. 12:2.

24 Marcus Noland and Tyler Moran, "Study: Firms with More Women in the C-Suite Are More Profitable," *Harvard Business Review*, February 8, 2016, https://hbr.org/2016/02/study-firms-with-more-women-in-the-c-suite-are-more-profitable.

25 Tara S. Mohr, "Why Women Don't Apply for Jobs Unless They're 100% Qualified," *Harvard Business Review*, August 25, 2014, https://hbr.org/2014/08/why-women-dont-apply-for-jobs-unless-theyre-100-qualified.

26 Laura Clark, "Teachers Give Lower Math Scores to Girls," *Smithsonian*, February 13, 2015, https://www.smithsonianmag.com/smart-news/teachers-give-lower-scores-math-when-they-know-theyre-grading-girls-180954253/.

27 Lou Strolger and Priyamvada Natarajan, "Doling Out *Hubble* Time with Dual-anonymous Evaluation," *Physics Today*, March 1, 2019, https://physicstoday.scitation.org/do/10.1063/PT.6.3.20190301a/full/.

28 Josh Terrel et al., "Gender Differences and Bias in Open Source: Pull Request Acceptance of Women versus Men," *PeerJ Preprints* 4 (July 2016), https://doi.org/10.7287/peerj.preprints.1733v2.

29 Chris Gaetano, "Woman Who Switched to Man's Name on Resume Goes From 0 to 70 Percent Response Rate," *The Trusted Professional*, June 8, 2016, https://www.nysscpa.org/news/publications/the-trusted-professional/article/woman-who-switched-to-man's-name-on-resume-goes-from-0-to-70-percent-response-rate-060816.

30 Advisory Board, "How Often Are Women Interrupted by Men? Here's What the Research Says," The Daily Briefing, July 7, 2017, https://www.advisory.com/en/daily-briefing/2017/07/07/men-interrupting-women.

31 Linda Babcock and Sara Laschever, *Women Don't Ask: Negotiation and the Gender Divide* (Princeton: Princeton University Press, 2004).

32 Babcock and Laschever, *Women Don't Ask*.

33 Tara Law, "Women Are Now the Majority of the U.S. Workforce — But Working Women Still Face Serious Challenges," *Time*, January 16, 2020, https://time.com/5766787/women-workforce/.

34 Col. 3:23–24.

35 2 Tim. 1:7; Matt. 11:28–30.

36 Ps. 37:3–5; Gal. 5:16.

37 Gen. 16, 18, 21.

38 Gen. 25–50.

39 Phil. 4:7.

40 Matt. 25:14–30; Prov. 28:2, 19; Luke 16:10–12.

41 Phil. 4:19; 1 Tim. 6:10.

42 Acts 20:35.

43 2 Cor. 9:7; Luke 6:38; Acts 20:35; Mark 12:41–44.

44 Deut. 24:14–15; Col. 4:1; Mal. 3:5; James 5:4; Jer. 22:13; Rom. 4:4.

45 Col. 3:23.

46 Sarah Kocher, "These Are the Most Popular Jobs Kids Dream of Doing When They Grow Up," SWNSdigital.com, December 19, 2019, https://swnsdigital.com/2019/12/these-are-the-most-popular-jobs-kids-dream-of-doing-when-they-grow-up/.

47 Fatherly, "The 2017 Imagination Report: What Kids Want to be When They Grow Up," *Fatherly*, December 22, 2017, https://www.fatherly.com/love-money/the-2017-imagination-report-what-kids-want-to-be-when-they-grow-up/.

48 "How to Ask for A Raise," *PayScale*, accessed October 10, 2021, https://www.payscale.com/data/how-to-ask-for-a-raise.

49 Babcock and Laschever, *Women Don't Ask*.

50 Ps. 75:6–7.

51 Rev. 3:7–13.

52 Col. 3:23–24.

53 1 Sam. 16:7; 1 Cor. 12.

54 1 Pet. 5:5–7.

55 "Brainwaves," NeuroHealth, accessed October 10, 2021, https://nhahealth.com/brainwaves-the-language/.

56 Amanda Gachot, "Understanding the Brainwaves of Your Children," Up All Hours, accessed October 16, 2021, https://upallhours.com/article/understanding-the-brainwaves-of-your-children.

57 "Brainwaves"; Gachot, "Understanding the Brainwaves."

58 "Brainwaves"; Gachot, "Understanding the Brainwaves."

59 "Brainwaves."

60 Jennifer Larson, "What to Know About Gamma Brain Waves," Healthline, June 22, 2020, https://www.healthline.com/health/gamma-brain-waves.

61 Ewen Callaway, "Fearful Memories Passed Down to Mouse Descendants," *Scientific American*, December 1, 2013, https://www.scientificamerican.com/article/fearful-memories-passed-down/.

62 Bruce Lipton, *The Biology of Belief 10th Anniversary Edition: Unleashing the Power of Consciousness, Matter & Miracles* (Carlsbad, CA: Hay House, 2016).

63 Heb. 11:1; Heb. 11:3; Matt. 21:21–22.

64 Gal. 5:22–23.

65 PeopleKeys, "Understand and Utilize the Predictible Behaviors of Your Team," *DISCInsights* (blog), 2018, https://blog.discinsights.com/understanding-different-types-of-employees-using-disc.

66 "Enneagram Population Distribution," Enneagram.bz, accessed October 15, 2021, https://enneagram.bz/en/test/stats/1-enneagram-population-distribution.

67 Gen. 1:1–3; 6–29.

68 Prov. 18:21.

69 CBS New York, "Student's Science Project Experiments on Bullying Plants," YouTube, May 15, 2019, video, 1:34, https://www.youtube.com/watch?v=yihMwoe8pV4.

70 ThisMomLovesIt, "Love/Hate Rice Experiment," YouTube, February 6, 2016, video, 2:13, https://www.youtube.com/watch?v=Kmo4Sh9IM1M.

71 Beyond Science, "Is Water ALIVE?! Water Responds to Our Words, Music & Even Thoughts," YouTube, November 14, 2015, video, 4:34, https://www.youtube.com/watch?v=IYRPy2G4TKs&t=59s.

72 Matt. 7:1–2.

73 Viktor E. Frankl, *Man's Search for Meaning* (London: Rider Books, 2020), 66.

74 "7 Ways to Remain Grateful All Year Long," *Amen Clinics* (blog), November 17, 2017, https://www.amenclinics.com/blog/7-ways-remain-grateful-year-long/.

75 "7 Ways to Remain."

76 Luke 6:45.

77 Matt. 13:18–23.

78 James 1:6–8.

79 "Recalling Hägg's 4:01.4 World Record Mile, on its 75th Anniversary," *World Athletics*, July 17, 2020, https://worldathletics.org/news/news/gunder-hagg-mile-world-record.

80 Bop Phillips, "The Sub-4 Alphabetic Register," Track & Field News, May 1, 2019, https://trackandfieldnews.com/wp-content/uploads/2019/05/Sub-4-Mile-Register-2019.pdf.

81 John 6:35, 41, 48, 51; 8:12; 10:7, 9, 11, 14; 11:25; 14:6; 15:1 NLT.

82 Rev. 3:20.

83 Phil. 2:6–7; John 14:9.

84 Jane Stevenson, "The New Playbook for Advancing Women in Leadership," *Korn Ferry*, April 2, 2021, https://www.kornferry.com/insights/this-week-in-leadership/the-new-playbook-for-advancing-women-leadership.

85 Joe Dispenza, *You Are the Placebo: Making Your Mind Matter* (Carlsbad, CA: Hay House, 2015), 67.

86 Christopher C. Evans, *Cancer Uncensored: Your Step-by-Step Guide to Cancer Prevention, Early Detection and Cancer Survival* (Lulu, Morrisville: 2012), 286.

87 Dispenza, *You Are the Placebo*, 40–41.

88 Matt. 14:22–33.

89 Martin L. Rossman, *Guided Imagery for Self-Healing: An Essential Resource for Anyone Seeking Wellness* (Novato, CA: H.J. Kramer, 2001), 193–198.

90 Gen. 1, 2.

91 Jude 20:21; Luke 4:1–13; Eph. 6:10–20; 1 Cor. 15:10; 2 Cor. 12:9; Phil. 3:3; James 4, 6.

92 2 Cor. 9:8; Ps. 90:17; Rom. 8:28; Prov. 16:9.

93 1 Sam. 17:37, 42–47.

94 Eph. 1:11; Ps. 5:12.

95 James 1:2; 2 Cor. 12:9–10; Phil. 2:1–23.

96 BW Online Bureau, "20 Minutes' Meditation Is Equivalent to 4–5 Hours of Deep Sleep, Say Experts at ASSOCHAM'S 'Illness to Wellness' Series," BW Education, December 31, 2020, http://bweducation.businessworld.in/article/20-Minutes-Meditation-Is-Equivalent-To-4-5-Hours-Of-Deep-Sleep-Say-Experts-At-ASSOCHAM-s-Illness-To-Wellness-Series/31-12-2020-360099/.

97 The results from using these tools are based entirely on my own personal experiences. Every individual is different, and no results are guaranteed. Please speak to a licensed medical professional before attempting to use any of the techniques outlined in this chapter.

98 Jim Richards, "Heart Physics® Coach Certification Course," 2020, https://heartphysics.com/coach-certification/.

99 Bradley Nelson, *The Emotion Code: How to Release Your Trapped Emotions for Abundant Health, Love, and Happiness* (New York: St. Martin's Essentials, 2019).

100 Gary Craig, "Official EFT Tutorial: Welcome to the Gold Standard (Official) EFT Tutorial," November 2019, https://www.emofree.com/english/eft-tapping-tutorial-en.html.

101 Elise Ackerman, "Superiority of Female Workers Confirmed: Study Finds Women Really Do Work Longer and Harder than Men," *Forbes*, February 24, 2013, https://www.forbes.com/sites/eliseackerman/2013/02/24/superiority-of-female-workers-confirmed-study-finds-women-really-do-work-longer-and-harder-than-men/?sh=43b6bc681770.

102 Douglas A. Wick, "Pre-Suade Customers and Employees to Change—Dr. Robert Cialdini—San Antonio Summit," *Strategic Discipline Blog*, June 1, 2017, https://strategicdiscipline.positioningsystems.com/blog-0/pre-suade-customers-and-employees-to-change-dr-robert-cialdini-san-antonio-summit.

103 Dan Sullivan, *The 80% Approach* (Toronto: The Strategic Coach, 2013).

104 Deut. 1:2; Num. 13:1, 14:38.

105 Marie Forleo, "Self-made Millionaire: The Simple Strategy that Helped Increase My Odds of Success by 42%," CNBC, September 13, 2019, https://www.cnbc.com/2019/09/13/self-made-millionaire-how-to-increase-your-odds-of-success-by-42-percent-marie-forleo.html.

106 James Collins, *Good to Great: Why Some Companies Make the Leap...and Others Don't* (New York: HarperCollins, 2001).

107 History.com Editors, "Ford's Assembly Line Starts Rolling," History.com, accessed October 10, 2021, https://www.history.com/this-day-in-history/fords-assembly-line-starts-rolling.

108 Michael Zhang, "What Kodak Said about Digital Photography in 1975," PetaPixel.com, September 21, 2017, https://petapixel.com/2017/09/21/kodak-said-digital-photography-1975/.

109 Zig Ziglar, "Thank You, Zig!" *Ziglar Pure and Simple* (blog), March 13, 2009, https://tziglar.wordpress.com/2009/03/13/thank-you-zig-ziglar-2/.

110 Elizabeth Dori Tunstall, "How Maya Angelou Made Me Feel," *The Conversation*, May 24, 2014, https://theconversation.com/how-maya-angelou-made-me-feel-27328.

111 Phil. 4:7.

Leadership Circles

Ready to Grow as a Leader?
Don't Go Alone!

Join our weekly Leadership Circles today!
My friend and mentor John Maxwell taught me that leadership is a journey and the journey is a lot more fun and rewarding when you share it with others. Leadership Circles allow you to accelerate your leadership and develop the most important skill - influencing others. When we are effective at leading, all areas of our lives are improved.

YOU WILL EXPERIENCE:

- Accelerated personal and professional growth
- Support and encouragement from a community of like-minded women
- Greater confidence
- Effective communication
- Better organizational outcomes for productivity and profitability
- The ability to grow high-performance teams
- Greater Emotional Intelligence

Leadership Circles are designed to be effective for women at all levels of the organization.

Find your circle of women today!
MaryGuirovich.com/LeadershipCircles

Lasting Transformation Starts In Your Heart

A limitless life is within reach when you discover the keys to removing your personal boundaries. You must go beyond knowledge to experience true connection and freedom. When you learn to open the door of your heart to God, you will experience effortless, positive, and everlasting transformation at the heart level.

When the door to your heart is opened, transformation becomes simple, and the limits are removed, allowing you to experience:

- Greater confidence, peace, hope, love, and joy, allowing God's grace to naturally prune stress, anger, self-doubt, and other negative emotions
- A deeper connection to God and the ability to hear His voice
- The unconditional love of God
- Unmovable Faith
- The ability to change your beliefs at the heart level
- A healthy sense of self-worth and dignity
- The reality of Christ in you

Start experiencing the promises of God today.

MaryGuirovich.com/HeartCourse

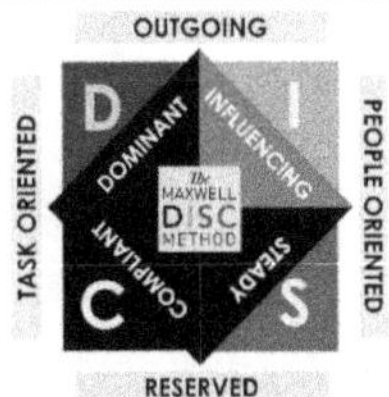

What if you could tap into your greatest motivations and dramatically improve your relationships and accelerate your results?

Your individual personality affects every aspect of your life. That's why one of the best things you can do to grow yourself and others is to understand your personality and what naturally drives you. When you recognize your strengths and weaknesses, you are able to give your best as you work with people around you.

THROUGH THE DISC PROFILE WORKSHOP YOU WILL EXPLORE WAYS TO:

- Apply the Law of Awareness to recognize your strengths and limitations
- Overcome your shortcomings and clear the path for personal and professional growth
- Understand how others are different and how to work with each personality
- Build a stronger team that communicates, appreciates the style of others and works well together
- Learn effective strategies for handling conflict and personality clashes
- Develop yourself and others to be their best

Take your DISC Assessment or Schedule a DISC Workshop for your company today!
MaryGuirovich.com/DISC

GET ALONG WITH EVERYONE, EVEN IF YOU'RE NOT A 'PEOPLE PERSON.'

LAW OF AWARENESS: YOU MUST KNOW YOURSELF TO GROW YOURSELF.

THE MARY GUIROVICH SHOW

Join Mary Every Week on the
Mary Guirovich Show

Connect with Mary in your pocket while commuting to work, on your lunch break, shuttling kids, burning calories, or around the house.

Every week Mary shares her latest lessons on leadership, career advancement, and life lessons from God. Listen in for holistic career strategies and interviews with inspirational guests to help you design a career and a life that you love. Mary hopes to provide encouragement every single time you listen!

YOU'LL BE INSPIRED TO:

- Achieve more in your career than you ever thought possible
- Accelerate your leadership and communication skills
- Gain confidence and clarity to design the life and career you want
- Lead with the grace of God at work, home, and in life

Subscribe to the Podcast at
MaryGuirovich.com/Podcast

Mary empowers and advocates for professional women and offers the practical, confidence-building advice women need to advance their careers and lead. Using action learning backed by deep research and authentic stories, her approach is forward-thinking, heart-centered, and creative, equipping today's women with tools they can use immediately.

HIGH DEMAND KEYNOTES

My Promotion Plan Blueprint- The 7 Steps to Career Advancement

Disrupting Everyday Gender Bias and Becoming a Champion

"Workship" God's Design for Women and Work

Legacy Leader-Building Teams With Impact

The #1 Killer of Your Compensation-(Get Hired and Negotiate Your First Salary)

"If you're looking for a speaker that is authentic, will take your leaders to the next level, and provide practical tools to reach their goals—look no further."

La Toya Gadson

Book Mary for your event at:
MaryGuirovich.com/speaking

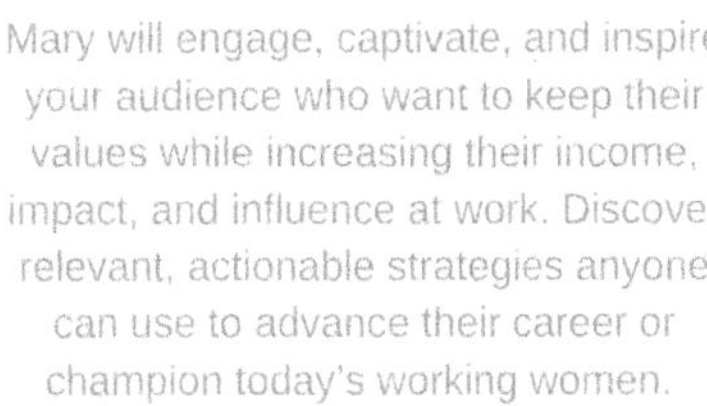

Mary will engage, captivate, and inspire your audience who want to keep their values while increasing their income, impact, and influence at work. Discover relevant, actionable strategies anyone can use to advance their career or champion today's working women.

Most popular audiences include professional women, business leaders and owners, college and university students and women of faith.

CPSIA information can be obtained
at www.ICGtesting.com
Printed in the USA
BVHW030930250222
629770BV00024B/803/J